EIGHTH EDITION

CLASSROOM READING INVENTORY

NICHOLAS J. SILVAROLI

Arizona State University

PUBLISHERS

Madison, WI Dubuque Guilford, CT Chicago Toronto London
Mexico City Caracas Buenos Aires Madrid Bogotá Sydney

Book Team

Executive Publisher *Edgar J. Laube*
Managing Editor *Sue Pulvermacher-Alt*
Developmental Editor *Suzanne M. Guinn*
Production Editor *Marilyn Rothenberger*
Proofreading Coordinator *Carrie Barker*
Art Editor *Rita Hingtgen*
Production Manager *Beth Kundert*
Production/Costing Manager *Sherry Padden*
Visuals/Design Freelance Specialist *Mary L. Christianson*
Marketing Manager *Amy Halloran*
Copywriter *Jennifer Smith*
Proofreader *Mary Svetlik Anderson*

Basal Text *10/12 Times Roman*
Display Type *Helvetica*
Typesetting System *Macintosh™ QuarkXPress™*
Paper Stock *50# Restore Cote*

Executive Vice President and General Manager *Bob McLaughlin*
Vice President, Business Manager *Russ Domeyer*
Vice President of Production and New Media Development *Victoria Putman*
National Sales Manager *Phil Rudder*
National Telesales Director *John Finn*

A Times Mirror Company

Cover and partial interior design by Tara Bazata

Cover background image © 1993 FotoSets

Copyedited by Anne Scroggin

Proofread by Wendy Christofel

Illustrations by Craig McFarland Brown and Jay Benson

Printed in the United States of America by Times Mirror Higher Education Group, Inc.,
2460 Kerper Boulevard, Dubuque, IA 52001

10 9 8 7 6 5 4 3 2 1

C O N T E N T S

FORM A

SPECIFIC INSTRUCTIONS: For Administering the Subskills Format   7

CRI INTERPRETATION: Subskills Format   13

SUBSKILLS FORMAT FORM A: Pretest   27

SUBSKILLS FORMAT FORM A: Posttest   63

FORM B

PREFACE

The Classroom Reading Inventory (CRI) is designed for in-service teachers and preservice teachers who have little or no experience with informal reading inventories.

To become better acquainted with my version of an informal reading inventory, the reader should:

1. Read the entire manual carefully.
2. Study the specific instructions thoroughly.
3. Administer the CRI to at least three students.
4. Keep in mind that skill in, and success with, individual diagnostic reading procedures is developed gradually through experience. Techniques, procedures, and ideas must be adapted to each testing situation. You will begin to gain confidence with the Classroom Reading Inventory after administering it seven to ten times.

This edition of the CRI is slightly different than earlier versions. In response to requests from users, Form A follows a subskills format, and Form B follows a reader response format. Both forms include pre tests and post tests. Form C includes diagnostic subskills material for high school and adult education students, and is available in a customized format through Brown & Benchmark. You can order a combination of these forms to create your own customized CRI. See page 3 for more information about this new structure.

I dedicate this edition of the Classroom Reading Inventory to my family: my mother, Caroline; my daughter, Diane, and her husband, Haamid; my daughter, Christine; my daughter, Pamela, and her husband, George; and to my first grandchild, Eleni.

To my friends and colleagues—Warren Wheelock, Lyndon Searfoss, and Robert Ruddell—my gratitude and indebtedness for their support and invaluable contributions to the development of this edition of the Classroom Reading Inventory.

Also, a special thank you to the following reviewers for their honest and insightful comments:

Diane E. Bushner
Salem State College
Janice R. Buswell
Metropolitan State College of Denver
Michael L. Tanner
Northern Arizona University
Scott Beesley
Grand Canyon College
Nancy E. Clements
Saint Francis College
Maryanne R. Bednar
La Salle University

Nicholas J. Silvaroli

INTRODUCTION

Purpose of the Classroom Reading Inventory

Norm-referenced tests (group reading tests) are used to determine student reading achievement. This group testing approach might be called classification testing. The results classify students according to a global reading achievement level, which is frequently interpreted as a student's instructional reading level. The Classroom Reading Inventory (CRI), a version of an informal reading inventory, is an individual testing procedure that attempts to identify a student's reading skills or abilities or both.

Differences Between Individual and Group Testing

The differences between individual and group testing can be illustrated by a brief description of the reading performances of two fifth-grade students, Joan and Don. Their norm-referenced test (NRT) results are:

Joan (10 years, 9 months old): NRT 4.2 overall reading
Don (11 years, 2 months old): NRT 4.2 overall reading

When we examine their NRT results, these two fifth-grade students appear to be about the same in age and overall reading achievement. However, data obtained from their individual CRIs indicate that there are significant *instructional* differences between these two students.

On the Graded Word Lists of Part 1, Joan correctly pronounced all the words at all the grade levels, one through eight inclusive. It is evident, therefore, that Joan is able to "sound out" or "decode" words. However, when Joan read the Graded Paragraphs of Part 2, she was unable to answer questions about these paragraphs even at a primer-reader-level of difficulty.

Don, on the other hand, was able to answer questions about these same paragraphs up to a second-grade-reader-level of difficulty. However, his phonetic and structural analysis, or decoding, skills were inadequate for his level of development.

The results obtained from an NRT concerning reading achievement tend to *classify* students as average, above average, or below average in terms of their reading achievement. Also, grade equivalent scores on an NRT may be six months to two years above a student's actual instructional level. Therefore, as teachers, we need much more specific information if we are to be able to develop meaningful *independent* and *instructional* reading programs for every student. The CRI is designed to provide teachers with just such specific and necessary information.

What Is the Classroom Reading Inventory (CRI)?

The CRI is a diagnostic reading test providing information to teachers that will enable them to make instructional decisions. It is designed to be used with elementary, junior high/middle school, high school, and adult education students. The CRI employs two main formats: SUBSKILLS FORMAT and READER RESPONSE FORMAT.

Subskills Format

At the elementary, junior high/middle school levels, the Subskills Format enables the teacher to diagnose a student's ability to decode words (word recognition) and to answer questions (comprehension). In addition, the Subskills Format provides both a pretest and posttest. The Subskills Format logically follows the type of reading instructional program being used in most elementary and junior high/middle schools.

Reader Response Format

A number of classroom reading programs have shifted from a subskills instructional emphasis to a literacy emphasis. The Reader Response Format follows the type of literacy program that challenges students to use their inferential and critical reading and thinking abilities. The Reader Response Format provides both a pretest and a posttest for use with elementary and junior high/middle school students.

Customized Format

This edition of the CRI *does not* include diagnostic subskills material for high school and adult education students as in earlier editions. However, diagnostic subskills material is available on a CUSTOMIZED basis and can be purchased directly from Brown and Benchmark Publishers. The decision to customize these forms and make them available through the publishers was made because high school and adult education programs are not likely to need elementary and junior high/middle school material. The reverse is also true. Therefore, this change enables us to reduce the cost of the CRI. To obtain a copy of the CUSTOMIZED CRI: FORM C Pretest & Posttest contact:

Brown and Benchmark Publishers
Educational Resources
2460 Kerper Blvd.
Dubuque, IA 52001–0539
1–800–338–5371

Brief Overview

What follows is a brief overview of the formats and forms used in the eighth edition of the CRI:

SUBSKILLS FORMAT (elementary, junior high/middle school)
    Form A: Pretest
    Form A: Posttest

READER RESPONSE FORMAT (elementary, junior high/middle school)
    Form B: Pretest
    Form B: Posttest

CUSTOMIZED SUBSKILLS FORMAT (high school and adult)
    Form C: Pretest
    Form C: Posttest

How Does the Subskills Format Differ from the Reader Response Format?

- SUBSKILLS FORMAT: The Subskills Format enables the teacher to evaluate the student's ability to decode words in and out of context and to evaluate the student's ability to answer factual/literal, vocabulary, and inference questions.
- READER RESPONSE FORMAT: The Reader Response Format enables the teacher to evaluate various aspects of the student's comprehension ability by means of the following procedure. First, the student is asked to use the picture and story title to *predict* what the story will be about. Second, the student is asked to *retell* the story or text with an emphasis on character(s), problem(s), and outcome(s)/solution(s).
- SUBSKILLS FORMAT: Both formats use a *quantitative* scale for the evaluation of a student's reading ability. In the Subskills Format, if the student answers correctly four of the five questions the student is considered to be *independent* in comprehension at that level. This format evaluates the student's ability to answer questions correctly.
- READER RESPONSE FORMAT: In the Reader Response Format, a number is assigned to the *quality* of the responses given by the student. If, for example, when the student is discussing character(s), the student is given zero credit for no response and three points if, in the teacher's judgment, the student's response is on target. The Reader Response Format is designed to enable the teacher to evaluate the student's ability to predict and retell narrative or expository texts.

Are There Other Differences?

- SUBSKILLS FORMAT: When using the Subskills Format the teacher tends to play a passive role. The teacher records correct and incorrect student responses and evaluates these responses to determine subskills needs in word recognition and comprehension.
- READER RESPONSE FORMAT: The Reader Response Format requires that the teacher play a more active role. For example, the teacher directs the student to make predictions about the story and asks the student to retell what s/he can about the character(s), problem(s), and outcome(s)/solution(s) of the story. The teacher evaluates the student's thinking in terms of how the student makes inferences and summarizes information, to mention just two examples.

Are There Ways in Which These Formats Are Similar?

Both the Subskills Format and the Reader Response Format provide the teacher with realistic information. Both formats establish instructional reading levels.

Is the CRI Used with Groups or Individuals?

Within both formats, all six forms are to be used with individual students.

What Is Meant by Background Knowledge Assessment?

A student's background knowledge plays a crucial part in the reading comprehension process. Taylor, Harris, and Pearson (1988) stated, "People comprehend reading material by relating the new information in the text to their background knowledge."[1] It follows that the teacher should make a quick assessment of the student's background knowledge before the student is asked to read any narrative or expository material. Furthermore, the teacher should consider the amount of background knowledge when determining the levels.

Why Are Administrative Time and Cost Important Factors in the CRI?

Teachers generally have only limited time to test individual students. With this in mind, each form of the CRI is designed to be administered in *fifteen minutes or less*. However, more time is needed when learning to give the CRI. Cost is kept to a minimum by permitting teachers to reproduce the Inventory Record for all six forms.

What Readability Formula Was Used in the Development of the CRI?

- For the Subskills Format-Form A: Pretest and Form A: Posttest, the Fry Readability Formula[2] was used. This is also the case for the Customized Subskills Format-Form C: Pretest and Form C: Posttest.
- For the Reader Response Format-Form B: Pretest and Form B: Posttest, a formula developed by Singer[3] called the SEER Technique was used.

1. Taylor, B., Harris, L., and Pearson, P. D. Reading Difficulties, Random House, NY, 1988, p. 226.

2. Fry, Edward B. *Reading Instruction for Classroom and Clinic.* McGraw-Hill Book Company, NY, 1972, pp. 230–234.

3. Singer, Harry. The SEER Technique: A Non-Computational Procedure for Quickly Estimating Readability Level, *Journal of Reading Behavior,* 1975, VII, p. 3.

A WORD TO THE WISE

1. When administering the Classroom Reading Inventory, a right-handed teacher seems to have better control of the testing situation by placing the student to the left, thus avoiding the problem of having the inventory record forms between them.

2. When administering Part 2 (Graded Paragraphs), the teacher should remove the student booklet before asking the questions on the comprehension check. Thus, the student is encouraged to utilize recall ability rather than merely locate answers in the material just read.

3. The word count given in parentheses at the top of each paragraph in the Inventory Record for Teachers does not include the words in the title.

4. Students living in different parts of the United States may react differently to the Graded Paragraphs. If you or your students react negatively to one or more of the paragraphs, feel free to interchange the paragraphs contained in the Pre- and Posttests.

5. It is important to establish rapport with the student being tested. Avoid using words such as "test" or "test taking." Instead use "working with words," "saying words for me," or "talking about stories."

6. Before the teacher can analyze the types of word recognition errors a student makes, s/he will need a basic understanding of the word recognition concepts listed on the Inventory Record Summary sheet; such as, blends, digraphs, short vowels. (See p. 49 for a reference regarding basic word recognition concepts.)

7. When a student hesitates or cannot pronounce a word in Part 2 (Graded Paragraphs), the teacher should *quickly* pronounce that word to maintain the flow of the oral reading.

8. Testing on the Graded Paragraphs of Form A, Part 2, should be discontinued when the student reaches the Frustration Level in *either* word recognition or comprehension.

9. The scoring guide on Form A: Pretest and Posttest, Part 2, of the Inventory Record for Teachers may cause some interpretation problems. As an example, let's look at the scoring guide for the story "Our Bus Ride" from Form A, Part 2—Primer.

SIG WR Errors		COMP Errors	
IND (Independent)	0	IND (Independent)	0–1
INST (Instructional)	2	INST (Instructional)	1½–2
FRUST (Frustration)	4+	FRUST (Frustration)	2½+

Should IND or INST be circled if a student makes one or two significant word recognition errors? It is the author's opinion that (a) if the student's comprehension is at the independent level, select the independent level for word recognition; (b) if in doubt, select the lowest level. This practice is referred to as *undercutting*. If the teacher undercuts or underestimates the student's instructional level, the chances of success at the initial point of instruction increase.

SPECIFIC INSTRUCTIONS

For Administering the Subskills Format
Form A: Pretest and Form A: Posttest

PART 1 Graded Word Lists: Subskills Format

Purpose: To identify specific word recognition errors and to estimate the approximate starting level at which the student begins reading the Graded Paragraphs in Part 2.

Procedure: Present the Graded Word Lists, starting at the preprimer (PP) level and say:

"I have some words on these lists, and I want you to say them out loud for me. If you come to a word you don't know, it's O.K. to say—'I don't know.' Just do the best you can."

Discontinue at the level at which the student mispronounces or indicates s/he does not know five of the twenty words at a particular grade level (75 percent). Each correct response is worth five points.

As the student pronounces the words at each level, the teacher should record all word responses on the Inventory Record for Teachers.[4] Corrected errors are counted as acceptable responses in Part 1. These recorded word responses may be analyzed later to determine specific word recognition needs.

How to Record Student Responses to the Graded Word Lists

1. came	*+*	The + sign means the student decoded the word "came" correctly.
2. garden	*graden*	The student decoded the word "garden" as "graden."
3. stood	*P*	The P means the student did not respond to the word "stood" and the teacher pronounced it to maintain an even flow.
4. there	*three*	Initially, the student decoded "there" as "three" but quickly corrected him/herself. This is a self-corrected error.

PART 2 Graded Paragraphs: Subskills Format

Purposes:
1. To estimate the student's independent and instructional reading levels. If necessary, to estimate the student's frustration and listening capacity levels (see p. 8 for levels).
2. To identify significant word recognition errors made during oral reading and to estimate the extent to which the student actually comprehends what s/he reads.

---

4. The Inventory Record for Teachers is a separate record form printed on standard 8 1/2- by-11-inch paper. *Note:* Teachers have the publisher's permission to reproduce all, or any part, of the Inventory Record for Teachers.

Procedure: Present the Graded Paragraphs starting at the highest level at which the student decoded correctly all twenty words on the Graded Word Lists, Part 1 and say:

"I have some stories here that I want you to read out loud to me. After you finish a story, I will ask you some questions about what you read."

Levels

What follows is a brief explanation of each of the four *levels* that apply to Subskills Format—Form A. These four levels are referred to as Independent (IND), Instructional (INST), Frustration (FRUST), and Listening Capacity (LC).

Independent Level

The teacher's first aim is to find the level at which the student reads comfortably.[5] The teacher will use the independent level estimate in selecting supplementary reading material, and the library and trade books students will read on their own. Since this is the type of reading students will be doing for personal recreation and information, it is important that the students be given reading material from which they can extract content without hazards of unfamiliar words and concepts.

Instructional Level

As the selections become more difficult, the student will reach a level at which s/he can read with at least 95 percent accuracy in word recognition and with 75 percent comprehension or better. At this level the student needs the teacher's help. This is the student's instructional level,[6] useful in determining the level of textbook that can be read with teacher guidance.

Note: Most classroom teachers tend to be most interested in the student's Independent (IND) and Instructional (INST) levels. However, the Frustration (FRUST) and Listening Capacity (LC) levels are included in the event the teacher feels the need to obtain such data.

Frustration Level

When the student reads a selection that is beyond recommended instructional level, the teacher may observe symptoms of frustration such as tension; excessive finger-pointing; and slow, halting word-by-word reading. Comprehension will be extremely poor; usually most of the concepts and questions are inaccurately discussed by the student. This represents a level that should be avoided when textbooks and supplementary reading material are being selected.

Listening Capacity Level

The teacher is asked to orally read more difficult selections to determine whether the student can understand and discuss what was heard at levels beyond the instructional level. It is assumed that the reading skills might be improved through further instruction, at least to the listening capacity level.

75% comp. instructional at this level go up if over 75%

Recording Word Recognition Errors

In 1982, Pikulski and Shanahan[7] reviewed research on informal reading inventories. One of their conclusions was: "errors should be analyzed both qualitatively and quantitatively."

5, 6. The actual number of significant word recognition and comprehension errors permissible at each graded level can be found in the separate inventory record for teachers.

7. Pikulski, John, and Shanahan, Timothy. "Informal Reading Inventories: A Critical Analysis" in *Approaches to Informal Evaluation of Reading.* John J. Pikulski and Timothy Shanahan, eds. Newark, Delaware: International Reading Association, 1982, p. 103.

In previous editions of the CRI, it was assumed that all word recognition errors were weighted equally. As such, the teacher was asked merely to *quantify* word recognition errors. This edition requires the teacher to deal not only with counting errors (quantitative) but to think about what the student is actually doing as s/he makes the error (qualitative).

In general, a word recognition error should be judged as *significant* (high-weighted) if the error impacts or interferes with the student's fluency or thought process. *Insignificant* (low-weighted) word recognition errors are minor alterations and do not interfere with student fluency or cognition; for example, student substitutes *a* for *the* before a noun or infrequently omits or adds a word ending.

The following examples are designed to enable teachers to make qualitative judgments of significant (high-weighted) and insignificant (low-weighted) word recognition errors. It is impossible, however, to account for all possibilities. Therefore, teachers are advised to use this information as a guide to establish their own criteria for developing a qualitative mindset by which to determine whether the word recognition errors are significant or insignificant.

Significant and Insignificant Word Recognition Errors

The CRI recognizes the following five common word recognition error types.

1. The student does not recognize a word and *needs teacher assistance*. This is symbolized by placing a $\mathcal{P}$ (for pronounced) over the word not recognized. This is always regarded as a significant error.

   Example: The $\overset{\mathcal{P}}{\text{turkey}}$ is a silly bird.

2. The student *omits* a word or part of a word. This is symbolized by drawing a circle around the omitted word or word part. Infrequent omissions are considered insignificant word recognition errors. Frequent omissions are significant.

   Example: The cat chased the bird⟨s⟩ OR It was a ⟨very⟩ hot day.

3. The student *substitutes* a word for the word as given. This is symbolized by drawing a faint line through the given word and then writing the word substituted above it. This type of error is judged to be significant if it impacts or interferes with fluency or cognition. However, it may also be judged as insignificant if it does not interfere with fluency or cognition.

   Example: *Significant:* Baby birds like to eat seeds and $\overset{g\'oin}{\text{grain}}$.

   Insignificant: He went to $\overset{a}{\text{the}}$ store. OR The children were lost in the $\overset{woods}{\text{forest}}$.

4. The student *inserts* a word into the body of the sentence. This is symbolized by the use of a caret (^) with the inserted word above the caret. Insertions are usually regarded as insignificant word recognition errors because they tend to embellish what the student is reading. However, if the insertion changes the meaning of what is being read it should be judged as significant.

   Example: *Insignificant:* The trees look $\overset{so}{\wedge}$ small.

   Significant: The trees $\overset{don't}{\wedge}$ look small.

5. The student *repeats* a word(s). This is symbolized by drawing an arc over the repeated word(s). Repetitions are usually considered to be insignificant errors because it is believed that the student is repeating an "easy" word(s) to gain time in decoding a more "difficult" word. However, excessive repetitions suggest the need for more reading practice, and they should be judged as significant.

   Example: *Insignificant:* The crowd at the rodeo stood up.

   Significant: They were bound for the salt springs near the . . .

As teachers become accustomed to thinking (qualitative) about why students make the errors they do, they will become more attuned to qualitative analysis of word recognition errors. As such, they will begin to better understand the decoding process and what mediates error behavior. The following are examples of enhanced awareness on the part of teachers regarding qualitative analysis.

This is an error of omission and an error of substitution. The first error, *omitted s,* caused the second error, substituting *is* for *are.* If the student did not substitute *is* for *are* language dissonance would occur.

Example: The bird̶s̶ *is* ~~are~~ singing.

This is two word substitution errors of a reversal of word order. These errors were caused by the first word *How.* How, at the beginning of a sentence, usually signals to the reader that it will be a question. This is just what the reader did; anticipated a question and made it into a question.

Example: How high *are we* ~~we are~~

Here two words are contracted because it is more natural to say *it's* than *it is.*

Example: *It's* ~~It is~~ a work car.

Remember, it's not a case of how many errors (quantitative) but, rather, what caused the errors (qualitative). The more you become accustomed to thinking about error behavior, the better you will be able to understand the decoding process.

Marking Word Recognition Errors on Graded Paragraphs

- Student does not recognize a word. Teacher pronounces the word for the student and marks it with a *P*.

Example: Elephants are *P* unusual animals.

- Student substitutes a word for the word as given. Teacher writes the substituted word above the given word.

Example: We are *riding* ~~ready~~ to go now.

- Student omits a word(s) or a word part. Teacher draws a circle around the omitted word(s) or word part.

Example: It was a (good) day for a ride.

Example: After week⒮ of hunting . . .

- Student inserts a word into the body of a sentence. Teacher uses a caret to show where the word was inserted.

Example: Mike was John's ∧ *best* friend.

- Student repeats a word(s). Teacher draws an arc over the repeated word(s).

Example: It was a good day for a ride.

Evaluating Comprehension Responses

After each graded paragraph the student is asked to answer five questions. The separate Inventory Record for Teachers labels questions as follows:

(F) Factual or Literal
(I) Inference
(V) Vocabulary

Suggested answers are listed after each question. However, these answers are to be read as guides or probable answers. The teacher must judge the adequacy of each response made by the student.

Partial credit is allowed for all student answers to questions. In most cases it is helpful to record student responses if they differ from the listed suggested responses.

Scoring Guide

What follows is the scoring guide used for the story "Electric Cars," fifth-grade level, Form A: Pretest.

Scoring Guide	Fifth		
SIG WR	Errors	COMP	Errors
IND	2	IND	0–1
INST	6	INST	1 ½–2
FRUST	11	FRUST	2½+

The scoring guide for this level, as well as all other levels in Part 2: Graded Paragraphs, uses error limits for the reader; in other words, Independent (IND), Instructional (INST), and Frustration (FRUST) reading levels.

As such, the guide suggests that when a student reads "Electric Cars" and makes two Significant (SIG) Word Recognition (WR) errors, the student is able to Independently (IND) decode typical fifth grade words. Six Significant (SIG) errors at this level suggest an Instructional (INST) level.[8] Eleven Significant word recognition errors suggest that the student is Frustrated (FRUST) in Word Recognition at this level. This same scoring rationale should be applied to the comprehension portion of the guide.

This guide is for the teacher to determine realistic independent and instructional levels. The student's responses to words and questions must be evaluated. The scoring guide is just that—a guide. The teacher makes the final diagnosis.

8. See page 8 for a discussion of these levels.

Summary of Specific Instructions

Step 1 Establish rapport. Don't be in a hurry to begin testing. Put the student at ease. Make him/her feel comfortable.

Step 2 Administer Part 1, Graded Word Lists. Begin testing at the Preprimer Level.

Step 3 Administer Part 2, Graded Paragraphs. Begin at the highest level on which the student knew all twenty words on Part 1, Graded Word Lists.

Step 4 Background Knowledge Assessment. Before starting a graded paragraph, engage the student in a brief discussion about the story to be read. Attempt to uncover what the student knows about the topic, and try to get the student to make predictions about the story. If the student has some background knowledge, rate the student as *adequate*. If little or no background knowledge is evident, mark as *inadequate*.

Step 5 Graded Paragraphs. Have the student read the selection out loud. Check to see that the student understands that s/he will be asked to answer questions after each selection.

Step 6 Ask the questions, and be sure to record the student's responses if they differ from suggested responses.

Step 7 On the Graded Paragraphs if the student reaches the frustration level in either word recognition or comprehension, or both, stop at that level.

Step 8 Complete the Inventory Record, and use the information garnered from the Graded Word Lists and the Graded Paragraphs to determine the estimated levels.

Step 9 Remember! It is the teacher that makes the final diagnosis (qualitative), not the number of errors recorded (quantitative).

CRI INTERPRETATION

Subskills Format
Form A: Pretest and Form A: Posttest

The Classroom Reading Inventory is designed to provide the teacher with a realistic estimate of the student's independent, instructional, frustration, and listening capacity levels in reading. However, merely identifying various reading levels is only slightly better than classifying the student on the basis of a norm-referenced test score.

The Classroom Reading Inventory is much more effective when the teacher is able to pinpoint consistent errors in word recognition or comprehension development, or both. The Classroom Reading Inventory should enable the teacher to answer these specific questions.

- Is the student having more difficulty with word recognition or comprehension skills?
- Does the student have equal difficulty with both word recognition and comprehension skills?
- If the student's difficulty is in the area of word recognition skills, are the problems with consonants, vowels, or syllables?
- If the student's difficulty is comprehension, are the problems with fact, inference, or vocabulary questions? Is s/he a word caller?
- Does the student appear to have other needs? Does the student appear to need glasses? Does the student appear to be anxious or withdrawn? Are high-interest/low-vocabulary reading materials needed?

The following are a sample CRI record and a CRI practice worksheet. These examples are designed to help the teacher gain information on the scoring and interpretation of the Classroom Reading Inventory. Such information should enable the teacher to deal effectively with the type of questions previously presented.

Sample CRI Record

Pamela T. is a fifth-grade student whose chronological age is ten years, six months. Her full scale I.Q., as measured by the Wechsler Intelligence Scale for Children-III is 98, giving Pamela a mental age of ten years, four months. In her class, Pamela is in the middle reading group. Her grade equivalency score in reading is 4.8, as measured by a group reading achievement test.

Pamela's teacher, Wilbur Millston, administered Form A: Pretest of the Classroom Reading Inventory to Pamela. Her Inventory Record and Summary Sheet follow on pages 14 to 20.

FORM A: Pretest Inventory Record _____

Summary Sheet

Student's Name ___Pamela T.___ Grade __5__ Age (Chronological) __10-6__

yrs. mos.

Date __2/15/96__ School __Central__ Administered by __W. Millston__

<table>
<tr><th colspan="3">Part 1
Word Lists</th><th colspan="4">Part 2
Graded Paragraphs</th></tr>
<tr><th>Grade
Level</th><th>Percent of
Words Correct</th><th>Word Recognition
Errors</th><th></th><th>SIG WR</th><th>Comp</th><th>L.C.</th></tr>
<tr><td>PP</td><td>100</td><td rowspan="2">Consonants</td><td>PP</td><td></td><td></td><td></td></tr>
<tr><td>P</td><td>100</td><td>P</td><td></td><td></td><td></td></tr>
<tr><td rowspan="2">1</td><td rowspan="2">100</td><td>_____ consonants
_____ blends</td><td>1</td><td>IND.</td><td>IND.</td><td></td></tr>
<tr><td>_____ digraphs
_____ endings</td><td>2</td><td>IND.</td><td>INST.</td><td></td></tr>
<tr><td rowspan="2">2</td><td rowspan="2">100</td><td>_____ compounds
_____ contractions</td><td>3</td><td>IND.</td><td>FRUST.</td><td></td></tr>
<tr><td>Vowels</td><td>4</td><td></td><td></td><td></td></tr>
<tr><td></td><td></td><td>_____ long
_____ short</td><td>5</td><td></td><td></td><td></td></tr>
<tr><td></td><td></td><td>_____ long/short oo
_____ vowel + r</td><td>6</td><td></td><td></td><td></td></tr>
<tr><td></td><td></td><td>_____ diphthong
_____ vowel comb.
_____ a + l or w</td><td>7</td><td></td><td></td><td></td></tr>
<tr><td>3</td><td>95</td><td>Syllable</td><td>8</td><td></td><td></td><td></td></tr>
<tr><td></td><td></td><td>_____ visual patterns
_____ prefix</td><td colspan="4">Estimated Levels</td></tr>
<tr><td>4</td><td>95</td><td>_____ suffix</td><td colspan="4"></td></tr>
<tr><td>5</td><td>95</td><td rowspan="4">Word Recognition
reinforcement and
Vocabulary
development</td><td colspan="4">Grade</td></tr>
<tr><td>6</td><td>75</td><td>Independent</td><td colspan="3">1</td></tr>
<tr><td>7</td><td></td><td>Instructional</td><td colspan="3">2 (range)</td></tr>
<tr><td>8</td><td></td><td>Frustration
Listening Capacity</td><td colspan="3">3
not determined</td></tr>
<tr><td colspan="3">Comp Errors
_____ Factual (F)
__✓__ Inference (I)
__✓__ Vocabulary (V)
__✓__ "Word Caller"
    (A student who
    reads without asso-
    ciating meaning)
_____ Poor Memory</td><td colspan="4">Summary of Specific Needs:
Comprehension Problems.
Needs help associating her experiences with
print. Pam also needs help with inference (I)
and vocabulary (V) questions.</td></tr>
</table>

Permission is granted by the publisher to reproduce pp. 49 through 61 (FORM A: Pretest)

FORM A: Pretest   Part 1   Graded Word Lists

PP		P		1		2	
1 this	✝	1 came	✝	1 new	✝	1 birthday	✝
2 her	✝	2 day	✝	2 leg	✝	2 free	✝
3 about	✝	3 big	✝	3 feet	✝	3 isn't	✝
4 to	✝	4 house	✝	4 hear	✝	4 beautiful	✝
5 are	✝	5 after	✝	5 food	✝	5 job	✝
6 you	✝	6 how	✝	6 learn	✝	6 elephant	✝
7 he	✝	7 put	✝	7 hat	✝	7 cowboy	✝
8 all	✝	8 other	✝	8 ice	✝	8 branch	✝
9 like	✝	9 went	✝	9 letter	✝	9 asleep	✝
10 could	✝	10 just	✝	10 green	✝	10 mice	✝
11 my		11 play		11 outside		11 corn	
12 said		12 many		12 happy		12 baseball	
13 was		13 trees		13 less		13 garden	
14 look		14 boy		14 drop		14 hall	
15 go		15 good		15 stopping		15 pet	
16 down		16 girl		16 grass		16 blows	
17 with		17 see		17 street		17 gray	
18 what		18 something		18 page		18 law	
19 been		19 little		19 ever		19 bat	
20 on		20 saw		20 let's		20 guess	
	100%		100%		100%		100%

Teacher Note: If the child misses five words in any column—stop Part 1. Begin Graded Paragraphs, Part 2 (Form A: Pretest), at the highest level in which the child recognized all twenty words. To save time, if the first ten words were correct, go on to the next list. If one of the words is missed, continue the entire list.

FORM A: Pretest   Part 1   Graded Word Lists

3		4		5		6	
1 distant	✓	1 drain	✓	1 moan	_man_	1 brisk	_bisk_
2 phone	✓	2 jug	✓	2 hymn	✓	2 nostrils	_P_
3 turkeys	✓	3 innocent	✓	3 bravely	✓	3 dispose	✓
4 bound	✓	4 relax	✓	4 instinct	✓	4 headlight	✓
5 chief	✓	5 goodness	✓	5 shrill	✓	5 psychology	✓
6 foolish	✓	6 seventeen	✓	6 jewel	✓	6 farthest	✓
7 engage	_enrage_	7 disturb	✓	7 onion	✓	7 wreath	_wrath_
8 glow	✓	8 glove	✓	8 register	✓	8 emptiness	✓
9 unhappy	✓	9 compass	✓	9 embarrass	✓	9 billows	✓
10 fully	✓	10 attractive	✓	10 graceful	✓	10 mob	✓
11 court	✓	11 impact	✓	11 cube	✓	11 biblical	✓
12 energy	✓	12 lettuce	✓	12 scar	✓	12 harpoon	✓
13 passenger	✓	13 operator	✓	13 muffled	✓	13 pounce	✓
14 shark	✓	14 regulation	_regulate_	14 pacing	✓	14 rumor	✓
15 vacation	✓	15 violet	✓	15 oars	✓	15 dazzle	✓
16 pencil	✓	16 settlers	✓	16 guarantee	✓	16 combustion	✓
17 labor	✓	17 polite	✓	17 thermometer	✓	17 hearth	_P_
18 decided	✓	18 internal	✓	18 zone	✓	18 mockingbird	✓
19 policy	✓	19 drama	✓	19 salmon	✓	19 ridiculous	_redeck-_
20 nail	✓	20 landscape	✓	20 magical	✓	20 widen	✓
	95%		95%		95%		75%

Teacher Note: If the child misses five words in any column—stop Part 1. Begin Graded Paragraphs, Part 2 (Form A: Pretest), at the highest level in which the child recognized all twenty words. To save time, if the first ten words were correct, go on to the next list. If one of the words is missed, continue the entire list.

FORM A: Pretest   Part 2/Level 1 (49 Words)

Background Knowledge Assessment: This story is about puppies. What can you tell me about puppies?

adequate ☒   inadequate ☐

Puppies

Puppies are fun to watch.

They are born with their eyes closed.

Their ears are closed, too.

This is why they use their smell and touch.

Puppies open their eyes and ears after two weeks.

By four weeks most puppies can bark.

Puppies grow up to make good pets.

Scoring Guide   First

SIG WR Errors	**Comp Errors**
IND 0	IND 0–1
INST 2	INST 1½ –2
FRUST 4+	FRUST 2½+

Comprehension Check

(F) 1. _+_ When puppies are born, are their eyes open or closed?
(Closed)

(F) 2. _+_ At birth, puppies must use their smell and touch. Why?
(Eyes closed or ears closed)

(F) 3. _+_ How long does it take for puppies to open their eyes and ears?
(Two weeks)

(F) 4. _+_ What can puppies do after four weeks?
(Bark)

(I) 5. *½* Why do you think puppies are fun to watch?
(They jump, run around, roll around)

They can bark

Background Knowledge Assessment: This story tells how to make a simple telephone. How often do you use the telephone?

adequate ☒   inadequate ☐

A Simple Telephone

You can make your own private telephone. You will need two empty tin cans and some string. The two cans must have the tops cut off. Punch a small hole in the bottom of each can. Push the string through the holes and tie the string ends in a knot. Give someone a can and ask them to move away. The string must be straight and tight. One of you should speak into the open end of the "telephone." The other person will hear the voice as it moves along the string. Now you have a "simple telephone."

Comprehension Check

(F) 1. _+_ Name two things you need to make a simple telephone.
(Cans and string)

(F) 2. _+_ What do you need to do to the cans?
(Cut tops off or punch a hole in bottoms, or both)

(I) 3. _+_ Why do you have to tie knots in the string?
(So string won't slip out of can)

(I) 4. _✓_ Why should the string be straight and tight?
(So voice can move along string)
Don't know

(I) 5. _½_ Why do you think two people must be far away from each other when they talk on the "phone"?
(They can hear each other without the phone)
· *easy to talk*

Scoring Guide   Second

SIG WR Errors		Comp Errors	
IND	2	IND	0–1
INST	5	INST	1½ –2
FRUST	10	FRUST	2½⁺

FORM A: Pretest   Part 2/Level 3 (96 Words)

Background Knowledge Assessment: What can you tell me about elephants?

adequate ☒   inadequate ☐

Strange Facts About Elephants

Elephants are unusual animals. They take showers by shooting a stream of water from their trunks. An elephant uses its trunk to carry heavy logs. Elephants also use their trunks to breathe, smell, and eat.

A (frightened) elephant can run at a speed of more than twenty-five miles per hour. On a long journey an elephant travels at about ten miles per hour. The gray skin of an elephant looks thick and strong. It's not—flies and other insects can bite into the skin.

When you go to the zoo, be sure to visit the elephants.

Comprehension Check

(F) 1. __+__ Tell two of the ways elephants use their trunks.
(Shoot) water, breathe, smell, eat, (carry logs)

(F) 2. __✓__ If frightened, an elephant can run at what speed?
(Twenty-five MPH)
Don't know

(I) 3. __✓__ The skin of an elephant is not as strong as it looks. How do you know this?
(Flies and insects can bite into the skin)
Don't know

(F) 4. __+__ How fast do elephants travel on long trips?
(Ten MPH)

(V) 5. __½__ What does the word journey mean?
(A long trip, travel)
to go — ?

Scoring Guide   Third

SIG WR Errors		Comp Errors	
(IND	2)	IND	0–1
INST	5	INST	1½ –2
FRUST	10	(FRUST	2½+)

Upon examination of Part 2 Graded Paragraphs, it appears that Pamela has a problem with comprehension. She seems to have difficulty with inference and vocabulary questions. There is no problem with her word recognition skills. Pamela is called a word caller. She can sound out almost any word presented to her. However, she does not associate meaning with the words she decodes.

Again, if you are unfamiliar with how children develop comprehension skills in reading or what is meant by the term *word caller*, it is recommended that you refer to the textbook by Searfoss and Readence, *Helping Children Learn to Read*.[9]

Note: Pamela began the Classroom Reading Inventory by responding to the Graded Word Lists in Part 1. Mr. Millston began Part 2 Graded Paragraphs at the last place Pamela had 100 percent, which was Level 2.

If Pamela had obtained IND in both WR and COMP, her teacher would go on to the Level 3 paragraph. Pamela was IND in WR and INST in COMP; therefore, her teacher dropped back to the point where IND was reached for both WR and COMP (primer reading level). Level 3 is Pamela's instructional level.

Teacher Note: The Graded Paragraphs were started at Level 2. This was the last level at which Pamela successfully pronounced all twenty words (100 percent) on Part 1, Graded Word Lists. She evidenced comprehension difficulty; therefore, lower levels of the Graded Paragraphs were used.

What follows is a practice exercise for Linda P. Linda P. is a third-grade student whose chronological age is nine years, three months. Her Inventory Record has been partially completed. Parts 1 and 2, Estimated Levels, Consistent Word Recognition Errors, Consistent Comprehension Errors, and Summary of Specific Needs have been left blank. Analyze the Classroom Reading Inventory for Form A: Pretest, Parts 1 and 2, located on pages 22–25. Complete her Summary Sheet and compare your responses with the author's responses on page 26.

9. Searfoss, Lynn, and Readence, John. *Helping Children Learn to Read,* 3rd Edition, Allyn & Bacon, 1994.

FORM A: Pretest   Inventory Record _____

Summary Sheet

Student's Name _____Linda P._____   Grade __3____   Age (Chronological) __9-3____
yrs. mos.

Date _____   School _____   Administered by _____

Part 1 Word Lists			Part 2 Graded Paragraphs		
Grade Level	Percent of Words Correct	Word Recognition Errors	SIG WR	Comp	L.C.

Part 1 Word Lists		Part 2 Graded Paragraphs			
Grade Level — Percent of Words Correct	**Word Recognition Errors**		SIG WR	Comp	L.C.

Part 1:

Grade Level	Percent of Words Correct
PP	_____
P	_____
1	_____
2	_____
3	_____
4	_____
5	_____
6	_____
7	_____
8	_____

Word Recognition Errors

Consonants

____ consonants
____ blends
____ digraphs
____ endings
____ compounds
____ contractions

Vowels

____ long
____ short
____ long/short oo
____ vowel + r
____ diphthong
____ vowel comb.
____ a + l or w

Syllable

____ visual patterns
____ prefix
____ suffix

Word Recognition reinforcement and Vocabulary development

Part 2 — Graded Paragraphs:

	SIG WR	Comp	L.C.
PP			
P			
1			
2			
3			
4			
5			
6			
7			
8			

Estimated Levels

	Grade
Independent	_____
Instructional	_____ (range)
Frustration	_____
Listening Capacity	_____

Comp Errors

____ Factual (F)
____ Inference (I)
____ Vocabulary (V)
____ "Word Caller"
    (A student who reads without associating meaning)
____ Poor Memory

Summary of Specific Needs:

FORM A: Pretest   Part 1   Graded Word Lists

PP		P		1		2	
1 this	+	1 came	+	1 new	+	1 birthday	+
2 her	+	2 day	+	2 leg	legs	2 free	+
3 about	+	3 big	+	3 feet	+	3 isn't	+
4 to	+	4 house	+	4 hear	+	4 beautiful	+
5 are	+	5 after	+	5 food	+	5 job	+
6 you	+	6 how	+	6 learn	+	6 elephant	+
7 he	+	7 put	+	7 hat	+	7 cowboy	cow-
8 all	+	8 other	P	8 ice	+	8 branch	+
9 like	+	9 went	+	9 letter	+	9 asleep	+
10 could	+	10 just	+	10 green	P	10 mice	+
11 my		11 play	+	11 outside	out-	11 corn	+
12 said		12 many	+	12 happy	+	12 baseball	+
13 was		13 trees	+	13 less	+	13 garden	grade
14 look		14 boy	+	14 drop	+	14 hall	+
15 go		15 good	+	15 stopping	+	15 pet	+
16 down		16 girl	+	16 grass	+	16 blows	bilow
17 with		17 see	+	17 street	P	17 gray	gay
18 what		18 something	+	18 page	+	18 law	+
19 been		19 little	+	19 ever	+	19 bat	but
20 on		20 saw	+	20 let's	+	20 guess	+
	100 %		95%		80 %		75%

Teacher Note: If the child misses five words in any column—stop Part 1. Begin Graded Paragraphs, Part 2 (Form A: Pretest), at the highest level in which the child recognized all twenty words. To save time, if the first ten words were correct, go on to the next list. If one of the words is missed, continue the entire list.

FORM A: Pretest   Part 2/Level PP (24 Words)

Background Knowledge Assessment:[10] This story is about two children and their play car. Tell me what you think the children are doing.

adequate $\boxed{X}$ inadequate $\boxed{}$

The Play Car

"See my play car," said Tom.

"It can go fast."

Ann said, "It's a big car."

"Yes," said Tom.

"Would you like a ride?"

Scoring Guide   Preprimer

SIG WR Errors		**Comp Errors**	
(IND)	0	(IND)	0–1
INST	1–2	INST	1½–2
FRUST	3+	FRUST	2½+

Comprehension Check

(F) 1. __✓__ What are the names of the boy and girl in the story?
(Tom and Ann)

(F) 2. __✓__ What were they talking about?
(The play car, etc.)

(F) 3. __✓__ Who owned the car?
(Tom)

(F) 4. __✓__ What did Ann (the girl) say about the car?
(Big car)

(I) 5. __✓__ Tell one thing that Tom might have liked about the car.
(It was fast, big.)

FORM A: Pretest   Part 2/Level P (39 Words)

Background Knowledge Assessment: Has your class ever taken a field trip? What can you tell about field trips?

adequate $\boxed{X}$ inadequate $\boxed{}$

Our Bus Ride

It was time to go to the farm.

"Get in the bus," said Mrs. Brown.

"We are ready to go now."

The children climbed into the bus.

Away went the bus.

It was a good day for a ride.

Scoring Guide   Preprimer

SIG WR Errors		**Comp Errors**	
(IND)	0	(IND)	0–1
INST	2	INST	1½–2
FRUST	4+	FRUST	2½+

Comprehension Check

(F) 1. __✓__ Where were they going?
(Farm)

(F) 2. __✓__ How were they going?
(By bus)

(I) 3. __✓__ Who was Mrs. Brown?
(Teacher or bus driver)

(F) 4. __✓__ How did the children know that it was time for the bus to leave?
(Mrs. Brown said, "We are ready to go now.")

(F) 5. __✓__ Was this bus ride taking place during the day or at night?
(Day)

---

10. See page 5 for a discussion of Background Knowledge Assessment.

FORM A: Pretest Part 2/Level 1 (49 Words)

Background Knowledge Assessment: This story is about puppies. What can you tell me about puppies?

adequate $\boxed{X}$ inadequate $\boxed{}$

Puppies

Puppies are fun to watch.

_P
They are born with their eyes closed.

Their ears are closed, too.

_P
This is why they use their smell and touch.

Puppies open their eyes and ears after two weeks.

By four weeks most puppies can bark.

little ∧Puppies grow up to make good pets.

Scoring Guide   First

SIG WR Errors		Comp Errors	
IND	0	IND	0–1
INST	2	INST	1½ –2
FRUST	4+	FRUST	2½+

(INST 2 circled; IND 0-1 circled under Comp Errors)

Comprehension Check

(F) 1. __+__ When puppies are born, are their eyes open or closed?
(Closed)

(F) 2. __+__ At birth, puppies must use their smell and touch. Why?
(Eyes closed or ears closed)

(F) 3. __+__ How long does it take for puppies to open their eyes and ears?
(Two weeks)

(F) 4. __√__ What can puppies do after four weeks?
(Bark)
walk

(I) 5. __+__ Why do you think puppies are fun to watch?
(They jump, run around, roll around)
they run and jump funny

FORM A: Pretest   Part 2/Level 2 (98 Words)

Background Knowledge Assessment: This story tells how to make a simple telephone. How often do you use the telephone?

adequate [X]   inadequate [ ]

A Simple Telephone

You can make your own private telephone. [*P* / *phone*] You will need two empty (tin) cans and some string. [*P*] The two cans must have the tops cut off. Punch a small hole in the bottom of each can. [*near*] Push the [*small*] ∧ string through (the)(holes) and tie the string ends in a knot. Give someone a can and ask them to move (away.) The string must be straight and tight. [*P*] One of you should speak into the open end of the "tele phone." [*phone*] The other person will hear the voice as it moves along the string. Now you have a "simple telephone." [*phone*]

Scoring Guide   Second

SIG WR Errors		Comp Errors	
IND	2	IND	0–1
INST	5	(INST	1½ –2)
(FRUST	10)	FRUST	2½⁺

Comprehension Check

(F) 1. __+__ Name two things you need to make a simple telephone.
(Cans and string)

(F) 2. __+__ What do you need to do to the cans?
(Cut tops off or punch a hole in bottoms, or both)

(I) 3. __+__ Why do you have to tie knots in the string?
(So string won't slip out of can)

(I) 4. __√__ Why should the string be straight and tight?
(So voice can move along string)
Don't know

(I) 5. __√__ Why do you think two people must be far away from each other when they talk on the "phone"?
(They can hear each other without the phone)
not sure

FORM A: Pretest Inventory Record

Summary Sheet

Student's Name ___Linda P.___ Grade ___3___ Age (Chronological) ___9-3___
yrs. mos.

Date _____ School _____ Administered by ___N. Silvaroli___

<table>
<tr><th colspan="3">Part 1
Word Lists</th><th colspan="3">Part 2
Graded Paragraphs</th></tr>
<tr><th>Grade
Level</th><th>Percent of
Words Correct</th><th>Word Recognition
Errors</th><th>SIG WR</th><th>Comp</th><th>L.C.</th></tr>
<tr><td>PP</td><td>100</td><td rowspan="2">Consonants

____ consonants</td><td>PP</td><td>IND</td><td>IND</td><td></td></tr>
<tr><td>P</td><td>95</td><td>P</td><td>IND</td><td>IND</td><td></td></tr>
<tr><td>1</td><td>80</td><td>✓ blends
____ digraphs
✓ endings</td><td>1</td><td>INST</td><td>IND</td><td></td></tr>
<tr><td rowspan="2">2</td><td rowspan="2">75</td><td>✓ compounds</td><td>2</td><td>FRUST</td><td>INST</td><td></td></tr>
<tr><td>✓ contractions</td><td>3</td><td></td><td></td><td></td></tr>
<tr><td></td><td></td><td rowspan="2">Vowels

____ long</td><td>4</td><td></td><td></td><td></td></tr>
<tr><td></td><td></td><td>5</td><td></td><td></td><td></td></tr>
<tr><td></td><td></td><td>____ short
____ long/short oo</td><td>6</td><td></td><td></td><td></td></tr>
<tr><td></td><td></td><td>____ vowel + r</td><td>7</td><td></td><td></td><td></td></tr>
<tr><td></td><td></td><td>____ diphthong
____ vowel comb.</td><td>8</td><td></td><td></td><td></td></tr>
<tr><td rowspan="2">3</td><td rowspan="2">_____</td><td>____ a + l or w

Syllable</td><td colspan="4" rowspan="5">Estimated Levels</td></tr>
<tr><td>____ visual patterns</td></tr>
<tr><td>4</td><td>_____</td><td>____ prefix</td></tr>
<tr><td>5</td><td>_____</td><td rowspan="2">____ suffix</td></tr>
<tr><td>6</td><td>_____</td></tr>
<tr><td>7</td><td>_____</td><td rowspan="2">Word Recognition
reinforcement and
Vocabulary
development</td><td colspan="4"></td></tr>
<tr><td>8</td><td>_____</td><td colspan="4"></td></tr>
</table>

Estimated Levels

		Grade
Independent		P
Instructional		1 (range)
Frustration		2
Listening Capacity		not determined

Comp Errors

____ Factual (F)
____ Inference (I)
____ Vocabulary (V)
____ "Word Caller"
   (A student who
   reads without asso-
   ciating meaning)
____ Poor Memory

Summary of Specific Needs:

See paragraph below for a discussion of Linda's reading needs.

Permission is granted by the publisher to reproduce pp. 49 through 61 (FORM A: Pretest)

Linda is having difficulty applying word recognition skills. She appears to understand consonants and digraphs but needs to learn to apply the remainder of the consonant, vowel, and syllable skills. Linda comprehends what she reads but might experience difficulty with inference questions. She has an independent (IND) level of primer (P). Therefore, she should be encouraged to read independently at this level.

SUBSKILLS FORMAT
FORM A: PRETEST

PART 1 Graded Word Lists

FORM A: Pretest   Graded Word Lists

1	this	1	came
2	her	2	day
3	about	3	big
4	to	4	house
5	are	5	after
6	you	6	how
7	he	7	put
8	all	8	other
9	like	9	went
10	could	10	just
11	my	11	play
12	said	12	many
13	was	13	trees
14	look	14	boy
15	go	15	good
16	down	16	girl
17	with	17	see
18	what	18	something
19	been	19	little
20	on	20	saw

FORM A: Pretest   Graded Word Lists

1 new	1 birthday
2 leg	2 free
3 feet	3 isn't
4 hear	4 beautiful
5 food	5 job
6 learn	6 elephant
7 hat	7 cowboy
8 ice	8 branch
9 letter	9 asleep
10 green	10 mice
11 outside	11 corn
12 happy	12 baseball
13 less	13 garden
14 drop	14 hall
15 stopping	15 pet
16 grass	16 blows
17 street	17 gray
18 page	18 law
19 ever	19 bat
20 let's	20 guess

FORM A: Pretest   Graded Word Lists

1 distant	1 drain
2 phone	2 jug
3 turkeys	3 innocent
4 bound	4 relax
5 chief	5 goodness
6 foolish	6 seventeen
7 engage	7 disturb
8 glow	8 glove
9 unhappy	9 compass
10 fully	10 attractive
11 court	11 impact
12 energy	12 lettuce
13 passenger	13 operator
14 shark	14 regulation
15 vacation	15 violet
16 pencil	16 settlers
17 labor	17 polite
18 decided	18 internal
19 policy	19 drama
20 nail	20 landscape

FORM A: Pretest   Graded Word Lists

1 moan	1 brisk
2 hymn	2 nostrils
3 bravely	3 dispose
4 instinct	4 headlight
5 shrill	5 psychology
6 jewel	6 farthest
7 onion	7 wreath
8 register	8 emptiness
9 embarrass	9 billows
10 graceful	10 mob
11 cube	11 biblical
12 scar	12 harpoon
13 muffled	13 pounce
14 pacing	14 rumor
15 oars	15 dazzle
16 guarantee	16 combustion
17 thermometer	17 hearth
18 zone	18 mockingbird
19 salmon	19 ridiculous
20 magical	20 widen

FORM A: Pretest   Graded Word Lists

1 proven	1 utilization
2 founder	2 valve
3 motivate	3 embodiment
4 glorify	4 kidnapper
5 adoption	5 offensive
6 popper	6 ghetto
7 nimble	7 profound
8 sanitation	8 discourse
9 unstable	9 impurity
10 dispatch	10 radiant
11 pompous	11 horrid
12 knapsack	12 vastly
13 bankruptcy	13 strenuous
14 geological	14 greedy
15 stockade	15 sanitation
16 kerchief	16 quartet
17 glisten	17 tonal
18 obtainable	18 engender
19 pyramid	19 scallop
20 basin	20 gradient

SUBSKILLS FORMAT
FORM A: PRETEST

PART 2 Graded Paragraphs

The Play Car

"See my play car," said Tom.
"It can go fast."
Ann said, "It's a big car."
"Yes," said Tom.
"Would you like a ride?"

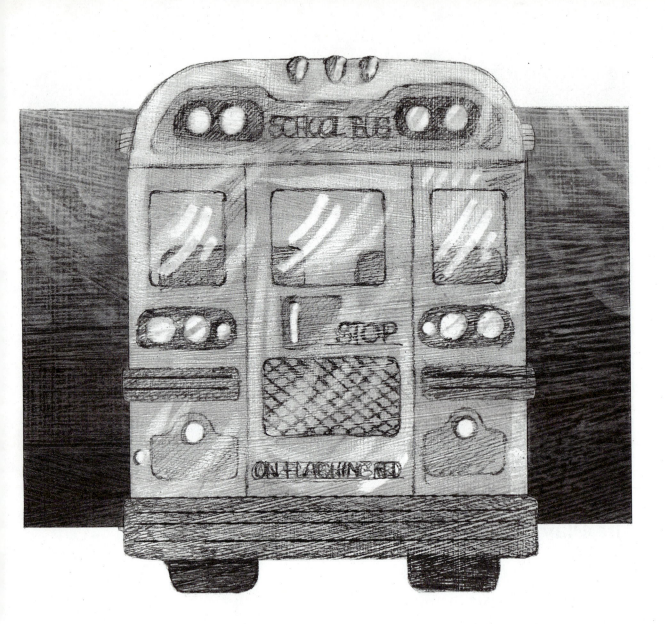

Our Bus Ride

It was time to go to the farm.
"Get in the bus," said Mrs. Brown.
"We are ready to go now."
The children climbed into the bus.
Away went the bus.
It was a good day for a ride.

Puppies

Puppies are fun to watch.
They are born with their eyes closed.
Their ears are closed, too.
This is why they use their smell and touch.
Puppies open their eyes and ears after two weeks.
By four weeks most puppies can bark.
Puppies grow up to make good pets.

A Simple Telephone

You can make your own private telephone.
You will need two empty tin cans and some string.
The two cans must have the tops cut off.
Punch a small hole in the bottom of each can.
Push the string through the holes and tie the string ends in a knot.
Give someone a can and ask them to move away.
The string must be straight and tight.
One of you should speak into the open end of the "telephone."
The other person will hear the voice as it moves along the string.
 Now you have a "simple telephone."

Strange Facts About Elephants

Elephants are unusual animals. They take showers by shooting a stream of water from their trunks. An elephant uses its trunk to carry heavy logs. Elephants also use their trunks to breathe, smell, and eat.

A frightened elephant can run at a speed of more than twenty-five miles per hour. On a long journey an elephant travels at about ten miles per hour. The gray skin of an elephant looks thick and strong. It's not—flies and other insects can bite into the skin.

When you go to the zoo, be sure to visit the elephants.

French Fried Tubers?

Tubers are another name for potatoes. Most potatoes are grown in Idaho, Maine, and New York. We like to bake, boil, mash, and French fry potatoes. We like French fries most of all.

Farmers must plant and pick their potatoes each year. Machines are used to dig up the potatoes from the soil. The potatoes are washed, peeled, and sliced. After they are fried in hot oil, they are frozen stiff and shipped to different places. Tons of French fries are prepared and sold each year.

How many times have you asked for a "hamburger and French fries"? Next time ask for French fried tubers.

Electric Cars

Will the cars of the future be electric cars? Many people hope so because electric cars might solve some of our pollution problems.

Electric cars have advantages and disadvantages.

Some advantages are: they do not produce exhaust fumes or use oil. They cost less and owners can recharge the batteries at home or at work.

Some disadvantages are: electric cars can travel only about 100 miles and then the batteries must be recharged. The batteries must be replaced over the lifetime of the car. Today's electric car can go only about sixty miles per hour.

Electric cars will not solve all of our problems, but they do seem to be our best hope for the future.

Blaze: Rebel Horse

All the ranchers in the valley knew about the wild stallion named Blaze, a powerful horse with a red mane. Many of the local cowboys tried to catch this rebel but failed each time. A reward was offered for his capture—dead or alive, because he encouraged other horses to run away with him.

Pete Cook and six other cowboys were determined to catch Blaze. Pete used binoculars to study the wild horse's movements. He made several maps of the valley and was sure he could capture Blaze this time.

Pete posted the cowboys along the secluded trails that Blaze usually followed. Each rider would pick up Blaze along the trail and force him into a narrow canyon, where Pete would be waiting.

The cowboys succeeded in forcing Blaze into the narrow canyon. Pete was ready with his rope, but Blaze came at him in a wild rage. Pete lost his balance but was able to roll over out of the way. Blaze saw his chance to escape and got away once again.

Salt Flat Speed

Rolling up to the starting line at Utah's Bonneville Salt Flats was a racing car that looked like something designed by Dr. Frankenstein on his day off. It had "Green Monster" emblazoned on its side. It was so ugly that some called it "the garbage truck." Over the huge jet intake on its nose was a short wing that looked like a coffee table. Bulging from its side was a cockpit in which the driver steered the car lying almost flat. But the Green Monster soon demonstrated that it was no "garbage truck."

Howling like a banshee, it streaked through the measured mile at 396 miles per hour. Then it turned around and sped back through the mile once more. This time the speed was 479 miles per hour. U.S. Auto Club officials checked their electronic timers and averaged the two runs. Art Arfons, the Green Monster's builder and driver, had set a new world's land-speed mark of 437.5 miles per hour! Racing cars now travel over 600 miles per hour.

Amazing Amelia

Amelia Earhart worked to open up new careers for women. She might easily qualify as an early feminist. When World War I ended, there were still a great many fields closed to women. Despite this, Amelia decided to go to medical school. In 1919 it was very difficult for women to get into medical school. Amelia persisted and did get into medical school. After her first year of school, Amelia decided to become a pilot.

After only ten hours of training, this amazing woman set a new world flying record. She flew to a height of over two miles.

Soon after this Amelia and an all-male crew made a flight across the Atlantic Ocean. This record-breaking flight took exactly twenty hours and forty minutes.

Until her death in 1937, Amelia continued to challenge many things that were thought to be impossible.

SUBSKILLS FORMAT
FORM A: PRETEST

Inventory Record for Teachers

FORM A: Pretest   Inventory Record _____

Summary Sheet

Student's Name _____ Grade _____ Age (Chronological) _____
yrs. mos.

Date _____ School _____ Administered by _____

Part 1 Word Lists			Part 2 Graded Paragraphs			
Grade Level	Percent of Words Correct	Word Recognition Errors		SIG WR	Comp	L.C.
PP	_____	**Consonants**	PP			
P	_____	_____ consonants _____ blends	P			
1	_____	_____ digraphs _____ endings	1			
		_____ compounds	2			
2	_____	_____ contractions	3			
		Vowels	4			
		_____ long	5			
		_____ short _____ long/short oo	6			
		_____ vowel + r	7			
		_____ diphthong _____ vowel comb. _____ a + l or w	8			

Estimated Levels

Grade Level	Percent of Words Correct	Word Recognition Errors
3	_____	**Syllable** _____ visual patterns _____ prefix _____ suffix
4 5 6 7 8	_____ _____ _____ _____ _____	Word Recognition reinforcement and Vocabulary development

	Grade
Independent	_____
Instructional	_____ (range)
Frustration	_____
Listening Capacity	_____

Comp Errors

_____ Factual (F)
_____ Inference (I)
_____ Vocabulary (V)
_____ "Word Caller"
    (A student who
    reads without asso-
    ciating meaning)
_____ Poor Memory

Summary of Specific Needs:

FORM A: Pretest Part 1 Graded Word Lists

PP		P		1		2	
1 this	_____	1 came	_____	1 new	_____	1 birthday	_____
2 her	_____	2 day	_____	2 leg	_____	2 free	_____
3 about	_____	3 big	_____	3 feet	_____	3 isn't	_____
4 to	_____	4 house	_____	4 hear	_____	4 beautiful	_____
5 are	_____	5 after	_____	5 food	_____	5 job	_____
6 you	_____	6 how	_____	6 learn	_____	6 elephant	_____
7 he	_____	7 put	_____	7 hat	_____	7 cowboy	_____
8 all	_____	8 other	_____	8 ice	_____	8 branch	_____
9 like	_____	9 went	_____	9 letter	_____	9 asleep	_____
10 could	_____	10 just	_____	10 green	_____	10 mice	_____
11 my	_____	11 play	_____	11 outside	_____	11 corn	_____
12 said	_____	12 many	_____	12 happy	_____	12 baseball	_____
13 was	_____	13 trees	_____	13 less	_____	13 garden	_____
14 look	_____	14 boy	_____	14 drop	_____	14 hall	_____
15 go	_____	15 good	_____	15 stopping	_____	15 pet	_____
16 down	_____	16 girl	_____	16 grass	_____	16 blows	_____
17 with	_____	17 see	_____	17 street	_____	17 gray	_____
18 what	_____	18 something	_____	18 page	_____	18 law	_____
19 been	_____	19 little	_____	19 ever	_____	19 bat	_____
20 on	_____	20 saw	_____	20 let's	_____	20 guess	_____
_____%		_____%		_____%		_____%	

Teacher Note: If the child misses five words in any column—stop Part 1. Begin Graded Paragraphs, Part 2 (Form A: Pretest), at the highest level in which the child recognized all twenty words. To save time, if the first ten words were correct, go on to the next list. If one of the words is missed, continue the entire list.

FORM A: Pretest   Part 1   Graded Word Lists

3		4		5		6	
1 distant	_____	1 drain	_____	1 moan	_____	1 brisk	_____
2 phone	_____	2 jug	_____	2 hymn	_____	2 nostrils	_____
3 turkeys	_____	3 innocent	_____	3 bravely	_____	3 dispose	_____
4 bound	_____	4 relax	_____	4 instinct	_____	4 headlight	_____
5 chief	_____	5 goodness	_____	5 shrill	_____	5 psychology	_____
6 foolish	_____	6 seventeen	_____	6 jewel	_____	6 farthest	_____
7 engage	_____	7 disturb	_____	7 onion	_____	7 wreath	_____
8 glow	_____	8 glove	_____	8 register	_____	8 emptiness	_____
9 unhappy	_____	9 compass	_____	9 embarrass	_____	9 billows	_____
10 fully	_____	10 attractive	_____	10 graceful	_____	10 mob	_____
11 court	_____	11 impact	_____	11 cube	_____	11 biblical	_____
12 energy	_____	12 lettuce	_____	12 scar	_____	12 harpoon	_____
13 passenger	_____	13 operator	_____	13 muffled	_____	13 pounce	_____
14 shark	_____	14 regulation	_____	14 pacing	_____	14 rumor	_____
15 vacation	_____	15 violet	_____	15 oars	_____	15 dazzle	_____
16 pencil	_____	16 settlers	_____	16 guarantee	_____	16 combustion	_____
17 labor	_____	17 polite	_____	17 thermometer	_____	17 hearth	_____
18 decided	_____	18 internal	_____	18 zone	_____	18 mockingbird	_____
19 policy	_____	19 drama	_____	19 salmon	_____	19 ridiculous	_____
20 nail	_____	20 landscape	_____	20 magical	_____	20 widen	_____
	_____ %		_____ %		_____ %		_____ %

Teacher Note: If the child misses five words in any column—stop Part 1. Begin Graded Paragraphs, Part 2 (Form A: Pretest), at the highest level in which the child recognized all twenty words. To save time, if the first ten words were correct, go on to the next list. If one of the words is missed, continue the entire list.

FORM A: Pretest   Part 1   Graded Word Lists

7

1 proven   _____

2 founder   _____

3 motivate   _____

4 glorify   _____

5 adoption   _____

6 popper   _____

7 nimble   _____

8 sanitation   _____

9 unstable   _____

10 dispatch   _____

11 pompous   _____

12 knapsack   _____

13 bankruptcy   _____

14 geological   _____

15 stockade   _____

16 kerchief   _____

17 glisten   _____

18 obtainable   _____

19 pyramid   _____

20 basin   _____

   _____ %

8

1 utilization   _____

2 valve   _____

3 embodiment   _____

4 kidnapper   _____

5 offensive   _____

6 ghetto   _____

7 profound   _____

8 discourse   _____

9 impurity   _____

10 radiant   _____

11 horrid   _____

12 vastly   _____

13 strenuous   _____

14 greedy   _____

15 sanitation   _____

16 quartet   _____

17 tonal   _____

18 engender   _____

19 scallop   _____

20 gradient   _____

   _____ %

Teacher Note: If the child misses five words in any column—stop Part 1. Begin Graded Paragraphs, Part 2 (Form A: Pretest), at the highest level in which the child recognized all twenty words. To save time, if the first ten words were correct, go on to the next list. If one of the words is missed, continue the entire list.

FORM A: Pretest   Part 2/Level PP (24 Words)

Background Knowledge Assessment:[11] This story is about two children and their play car. Tell me what you think the children are doing.

adequate ☐   inadequate ☐

The Play Car

"See my play car," said Tom.

"It can go fast."

Ann said, "It's a big car."

"Yes," said Tom.

"Would you like a ride?"

Scoring Guide   Preprimer

SIG WR Errors		COMP Errors	
IND	0	IND	0–1
INST	1–2	INST	1½–2
FRUST	3+	FRUST	2½+

Comprehension Check

(F) 1. ____ What are the names of the boy and girl in the story?
(Tom and Ann)

(F) 2. ____ What were they talking about?
(The play car, etc.)

(F) 3. ____ Who owned the car?
(Tom)

(F) 4. ____ What did Ann (the girl) say about the car?
(Big car)

(I) 5. ____ What do you think Tom might have liked about the car.
(It was fast, big.)

FORM A: Pretest   Part 2/Level P (39 Words)

Background Knowledge Assessment: Has your class ever taken a field trip? What can you tell about field trips?

adequate ☐   inadequate ☐

Our Bus Ride

It was time to go to the farm.

"Get in the bus," said Mrs. Brown.

"We are ready to go now."

The children climbed into the bus.

Away went the bus.

It was a good day for a ride.

Scoring Guide   Primer

SIG WR Errors		COMP Errors	
IND	0	IND	0–1
INST	2	INST	1½–2
FRUST	4+	FRUST	2½+

Comprehension Check

(F) 1. ____ Where were they going?
(Farm)

(F) 2. ____ How were they going?
(By bus)

(I) 3. ____ Who do you think Mrs. Brown was?
(Teacher or bus driver)

(F) 4. ____ How did the children know that it was time for the bus to leave?
(Mrs. Brown said, "We are ready to go now.")

(F) 5. ____ Was this bus ride taking place during the day or at night?
(Day)

---

11. See page 5 for a discussion of Background Knowledge Assessment.

FORM A: Pretest   Part 2/Level 1 (49 Words)

Background Knowledge Assessment: This story is about puppies. What can you tell me about puppies?

adequate ☐   inadequate ☐

Puppies

Puppies are fun to watch.

They are born with their eyes closed.

Their ears are closed, too.

This is why they use their smell and touch.

Puppies open their eyes and ears after two weeks.

By four weeks most puppies can bark.

Puppies grow up to make good pets.

Scoring Guide   First

SIG WR Errors	**COMP Errors**
IND 0	IND 0–1
INST 2	INST 1½ –2
FRUST 4⁺	FRUST 2½⁺

Comprehension Check

(F) 1. _____ When puppies are born, are their eyes open or closed?
(Closed)

(F) 2. _____ At birth, puppies must use their smell and touch. Why?
(Eyes closed or ears closed)

(F) 3. _____ How long does it take for puppies to open their eyes and ears?
(Two weeks)

(F) 4. _____ What can puppies do after four weeks?
(Bark)

(I) 5. _____ Why do you think puppies are fun to watch?
(They jump, run around, roll around)

FORM A: Pretest   Part 2/Level 2 (98 Words)

Background Knowledge Assessment: This story tells how to make a simple telephone. How often do you use the telephone?

adequate ☐   inadequate ☐

A Simple Telephone

You can make your own private telephone. You will need two empty tin cans and some string. The two cans must have the tops cut off. Punch a small hole in the bottom of each can. Push the string through the holes and tie the string ends in a knot. Give someone a can and ask them to move away. The string must be straight and tight. One of you should speak into the open end of the "telephone." The other person will hear the voice as it moves along the string. Now you have a "simple telephone."

Scoring Guide   Second

SIG WR Errors		**COMP Errors**	
IND	2	IND	0–1
INST	5	INST	1½ –2
FRUST	10	FRUST	2½⁺

Comprehension Check

(F) 1. _____ Name two things you need to make a simple telephone.
(Cans and string)

(F) 2. _____ What do you need to do to the cans?
(Cut tops off or punch a hole in bottoms, or both)

(I) 3. _____ Why do you have to tie knots in the string?
(So string won't slip out of can)

(I) 4. _____ Why should the string be straight and tight?
(So voice can move along string)

(I) 5. _____ Why do you think two people must be far away from each other when they talk on the "phone"?
(They can hear each other without the phone)

FORM A: Pretest   Part 2/Level 3 (96 Words)

Background Knowledge Assessment: What can you tell me about elephants?

adequate ☐   inadequate ☐

Strange Facts About Elephants

Elephants are unusual animals. They take showers by shooting a stream of water from their trunks. An elephant uses its trunk to carry heavy logs. Elephants also use their trunks to breathe, smell, and eat.

A frightened elephant can run at a speed of more than twenty-five miles per hour. On a long journey an elephant travels at about ten miles per hour. The gray skin of an elephant looks thick and strong. It's not—flies and other insects can bite into the skin.

When you go to the zoo, be sure to visit the elephants.

Comprehension Check

(F) 1. _____ Tell two of the ways elephants use their trunks.
(Shoot water, breathe, smell, eat, carry logs)

(F) 2. _____ If frightened, an elephant can run at what speed?
(Twenty-five MPH)

(I) 3. _____ The skin of an elephant is not as strong as it looks. How do you know this?
(Flies and insects can bite into the skin)

(F) 4. _____ How fast do elephants travel on long trips?
(Ten MPH)

(V) 5. _____ What does the word journey mean?
(A long trip, travel)

Scoring Guide   Third

SIG WR Errors		**COMP Errors**	
IND	2	IND	0–1
INST	5	INST	1½–2
FRUST	10	FRUST	2½+

FORM A: Pretest Part 2/Level 4 (105 Words)

Background Knowledge Assessment: Do you like to eat potatoes? How do you like them cooked? Tell me more.

adequate ☐   inadequate ☐

French Fried Tubers?

Tubers are another name for potatoes. Most potatoes are grown in Idaho, Maine, and New York. We like to bake, boil, mash, and French fry potatoes. We like French fries most of all.

Farmers must plant and pick their potatoes each year. Machines are used to dig up the potatoes from the soil. The potatoes are washed, peeled, and sliced. After they are fried in hot oil, they are frozen stiff and shipped to different places. Tons of French fries are prepared and sold each year.

How many times have you asked for a "hamburger and French fries"? Next time ask for French fried tubers.

Comprehension Check

(F) 1. _____ What is another name for potatoes?
(Tubers)

(F) 2. _____ What kind of potatoes do most people like to eat?
(French fried potatoes)

(I) 3. _____ Do potatoes grow above or below the ground?
(Below)

(V) 4. _____ What does prepared mean?
(Make ready, put in condition for something)

(F) 5. _____ Name one of the states where most potatoes are grown.
(Idaho, Maine, or New York)

Scoring Guide Fourth

SIG WR Errors		**COMP Errors**	
IND	2	IND	0–1
INST	6	INST	1½ –2
FRUST	11	FRUST	2½⁺

FORM A: Pretest Part 2/Level 5 (116 Words)

Background Knowledge Assessment: What can you tell me about electric cars?

adequate ☐ inadequate ☐

Electric Cars

Will the cars of the future be electric cars? Many people hope so because electric cars might solve some of our pollution problems.

Electric cars have advantages and disadvantages.

Some advantages are: they do not produce exhaust fumes or use oil. They cost less and owners can recharge the batteries at home or at work.

Some disadvantages are: electric cars can travel only about 100 miles and then the batteries must be recharged. The batteries must be replaced over the lifetime of the car. Today's electric car can go only about sixty miles per hour.

Electric cars will not solve all of our problems, but they do seem to be our best hope for the future.

Comprehension Check

(V) 1. _____ What word was used that means unclean air or fuel exhaust?
(Pollution)

(F) 2. _____ Give me some advantages for using electric cars.
(No exhaust, do not use oil, costs less, batteries easily charged)

(F) 3. _____ Give me some disadvantages.
(Can only travel 100 miles, batteries need to be replaced, top speed sixty MPH)

(I) 4. _____ How would electric cars reduce or solve some of our problems?
(Reduce pollution, less need for oil)

(I) 5. _____ What might happen if we continue to pollute the environment?
(Poor health, run out of oil, we might die)

Scoring Guide Fifth

SIG WR Errors		**COMP Errors**	
IND	2	IND	0–1
INST	6	INST	1½ –2
FRUST	11	FRUST	2½+

FORM A: Pretest   Part 2/Level 6 (174 Words)

Background Knowledge Assessment: This story tells about how a group of cowboys attempted to capture a wild horse. What are some things these cowboys would have to do to capture this wild horse?

adequate ☐   inadequate ☐

Blaze: Rebel Horse

All the ranchers in the valley knew about the wild stallion named Blaze, a powerful horse with a red mane. Many of the local cowboys tried to catch this rebel but failed each time. A reward was offered for his capture—dead or alive, because he encouraged other horses to run away with him.

Pete Cook and six other cowboys were determined to catch Blaze. Pete used binoculars to study the wild horse's movements. He made several maps of the valley and was sure he could capture Blaze this time.

Pete posted the cowboys along the secluded trails that Blaze usually followed. Each rider would pick up Blaze along the trail and force him into a narrow canyon, where Pete would be waiting.

The cowboys succeeded in forcing Blaze into the narrow canyon. Pete was ready with his rope, but Blaze came at him in a wild rage. Pete lost his balance but was able to roll over out of the way. Blaze saw his chance to escape and got away once again.

Comprehension Check

(F) 1. _____ Why did the ranchers want the wild horse (Blaze) captured?
(He encouraged other horses to run away.)

(F) 2. _____ What did the wild horse (Blaze) look like?
(Powerful, big, red mane)

(F) 3. _____ What did Pete Cook do before attempting to capture Blaze?
(He made maps of the valley and of the horse's trails.)

(V) 4. _____ What does "secluded" mean?
(Hidden, secret, hard to find)

(I) 5. _____ Describe how you think Pete's cowboys worked to capture Blaze.
(They spread out and forced him into a narrow canyon, they teamed up)

Scoring Guide   Sixth

SIG WR Errors		**COMP Errors**	
IND	3	IND	0–1
INST	8	INST	1½–2
FRUST	17	FRUST	2½+

FORM A: Pretest   Part 2/Level 7 (172 Words)

Background Knowledge Assessment: Fast cars are interesting to some people. Highways are designed to allow cars to travel at fifty-five miles per hour. Imagine a car that traveled faster than 600 mph.

adequate ☐   inadequate ☐

Salt Flat Speed

Rolling up to the starting line at Utah's Bonneville Salt Flats was a racing car that looked like something designed by Dr. Frankenstein on his day off. It had "Green Monster" emblazoned on its side. It was so ugly that some called it "the garbage truck." Over the huge jet intake on its nose was a short wing that looked like a coffee table. Bulging from its side was a cockpit in which the driver steered the car lying almost flat. But the Green Monster soon demonstrated that it was no "garbage truck."

Howling like a banshee, it streaked through the measured mile at 396 miles per hour. Then it turned around and sped back through the mile once more. This time the speed was 479 miles per hour. U.S. Auto Club officials checked their electronic timers and averaged the two runs. Art Arfons, the Green Monster's builder and driver, had set a new world's land-speed mark of 437.5 miles per hour! Racing cars now travel over 600 miles per hour.

Comprehension Check

(F) 1. _____ What was the name of this car?
(Green Monster)

(F) 2. _____ Why did some people call this car a "garbage truck"?
(Because it was ugly, because they didn't think it could set a record)

(F) 3. _____ What did the race car have over its jet intake on the nose of the car?
(A short wing)

(V)4. _____ The words "howled like a banshee" were used in this selection. What does that mean?
(A wailing, screeching, eerie noise)

(I) 5. _____ Why won't we see the Green Monster or a car like it driving along our streets?
(Car is too fast)

Scoring Guide   Seventh

SIG WR Errors		**COMP Errors**	
IND	3	IND	0–1
INST	7–8	INST	1½ –2
FRUST	15	FRUST	2½+

FORM A: Pretest   Part 2/Level 8 (143 Words)

Background Knowledge Assessment: Amelia Earhart was a courageous pioneer. Read these paragraphs to learn more about this courageous woman.

adequate ☐   inadequate ☐

Amazing Amelia

Amelia Earhart worked to open up new careers for women. She might easily qualify as an early feminist. When World War I ended, there were still a great many fields closed to women. Despite this, Amelia decided to go to medical school. In 1919 it was very difficult for women to get into medical school. Amelia persisted and did get into medical school. After her first year of school, Amelia decided to become a pilot.

After only ten hours of training, this amazing woman set a new world flying record. She flew to a height of over two miles.

Soon after this, Amelia and an all-male crew made a flight across the Atlantic Ocean. This record-breaking flight took exactly twenty hours and forty minutes.

Until her death in 1937, Amelia continued to challenge many things that were thought to be impossible.

Comprehension Check

(F) 1. _____ Why did Amelia leave medical college?
(To become a pilot, didn't like medical college)

(V) 2. _____ What does "feminist" mean?
(A person who is attempting to provide equal opportunities for women)

(F) 3. _____ How high did Amelia fly when she set a new world record?
(Over two miles)

(V) 4. _____ The word persisted was used. What does "persisted" mean?
(Refused to give up, to endure, etc.)

(I) 5. _____ What do you think is meant by this statement: "Amelia challenged the impossible"?
(She tried to break the world flying records. She wanted new opportunities for women, etc.)

Scoring Guide   Eighth

SIG WR Errors		**COMP Errors**	
IND	3	IND	0–1
INST	7	INST	1½ –2
FRUST	14	FRUST	2½⁺

SUBSKILLS FORMAT
FORM A: POSTTEST

PART 1 Graded Word Lists

FORM A: Posttest Graded Word Lists

1 in		1 three
2 now		2 find
3 so		3 because
4 from		4 head
5 get		5 their
6 had		6 before
7 at		7 more
8 over		8 turn
9 of		9 think
10 into		10 call
11 no		11 these
12 came		12 school
13 but		13 word
14 has		14 even
15 if		15 would
16 as		16 ask
17 have		17 much
18 be		18 want
19 or		19 never
20 an		20 your

FORM A: Posttest   Graded Word Lists

1 maybe	1 sound
2 pass	2 climb
3 out	3 waiting
4 they	4 hands
5 please	5 cry
6 love	6 doctor
7 cannot	7 people
8 eight	8 everyone
9 kind	9 strong
10 read	10 inch
11 paid	11 rock
12 open	12 sea
13 top	13 thirty
14 pool	14 dance
15 low	15 test
16 late	16 hard
17 giant	17 dogs
18 short	18 story
19 upon	19 city
20 us	20 push

FORM A: Posttest Graded Word Lists

1 computer	1 spy
2 angry	2 downtown
3 energy	3 tray
4 choice	4 lung
5 hospital	5 exhibit
6 court	6 formal
7 heard	7 weekend
8 closet	8 nineteen
9 meet	9 mixture
10 picnic	10 invitation
11 against	11 happiness
12 law	12 gulf
13 build	13 rumble
14 objects	14 plot
15 probably	15 tennis
16 shot	16 weary
17 we'll	17 lantern
18 paragraph	18 preparation
19 telephone	19 weep
20 sugar	20 jelly

FORM A: Posttest   Graded Word Lists

1 sensation	1 radiant
2 analyze	2 greatness
3 funeral	3 tardy
4 scissors	4 doughnut
5 mutual	5 armor
6 consistent	6 nurture
7 deliberately	7 dismay
8 officially	8 shipment
9 taxi	9 logic
10 parachute	10 pulley
11 radar	11 fingerprint
12 intermediate	12 jumbo
13 embarrass	13 guppy
14 raid	14 narrator
15 crude	15 crutch
16 bakery	16 shopper
17 knelt	17 punish
18 endure	18 silken
19 painful	19 omelet
20 squash	20 miniature

FORM A: Posttest   Graded Word Lists

1 noisily	1 duly
2 imperative	2 furnishing
3 forge	3 emptiness
4 expressway	4 frustration
5 nominate	5 joyously
6 include	6 patriotic
7 formulate	7 zeal
8 enact	8 seriousness
9 depot	9 notorious
10 illegal	10 federation
11 distress	11 youth
12 childish	12 selection
13 unfair	13 bleak
14 sentimental	14 mutton
15 designer	15 habitation
16 luggage	16 fling
17 historically	17 dungeon
18 uncertainty	18 hierarchy
19 gardener	19 duration
20 enchant	20 journalist

SUBSKILLS FORMAT
FORM A: POSTTEST

PART 2 Graded Paragraphs

The Work Car

"Look over there," said Jane.
"See the funny little car.
Can you see it?"
"I see it," said Bob.
"It is a work car."

Jack's First Airplane Ride

Jack and his father got on an airplane.

Away they flew.

"We are up high," said Jack.

"The trees look small."

"And so do the houses," said Father.

Jack said, "This is fun!"

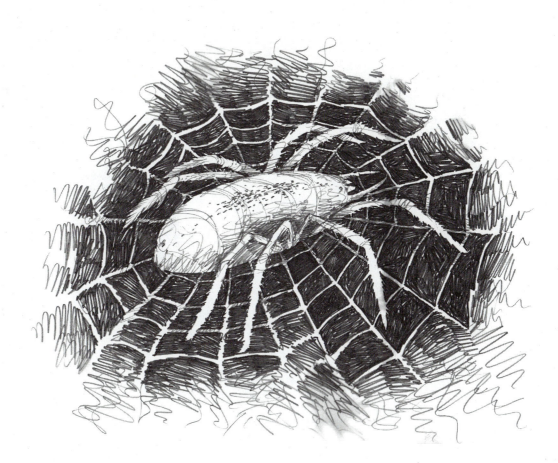

Plant Spiders

There are all kinds of spiders.
This black and green one is called a plant spider.
A plant spider has small feet.
All spiders have small feet.
Plant spiders live in nests.
They soon learn to hunt for food and build new nests.

The Rodeo

The people at the rodeo stood up.
They were all waiting for the big ride.
Everyone came to see Bob Hill ride Midnight.
Bob Hill is a top rider.
Midnight is the best horse in the rodeo.
He is big and fast. Midnight is a strong black horse.
Can Bob Hill ride this great horse?

Silly Birds

Even with food all around, baby turkeys will not eat. Turkeys can really be called "silly birds." Many die from lack of food. Straw is kept in their houses but some never seem to discover what it is used for. We will never understand senseless turkeys.

The silly young birds don't know enough to come out of the cold, either. So many get sick and die. If they see anything bright, they try to eat it. It may be a pencil, a small nail, or even a shovel. You can see how foolish these "silly birds" are.

Sky Diving

An exciting sport is sky diving. Sky divers do tricks, make falls, and take interesting pictures. This sport takes you away from your everyday life into a wonderful world you have never known. It is almost like being in a dream. Once out of the airplane, you feel as if you can climb walls or float over mountains.

Sky divers work to develop each of their jumps. Men and women are interested in sky diving. In fact, more people are learning to sky dive each year. This relaxing sport is one of people's adventures.

The Ground Cuckoo

The ground cuckoo is an unusual bird. It is about twenty-four inches long, including its long tail. It also has a long beak and a crested head. You can find it in the southwestern states.

This bird is helpful to people in many ways. It catches small lizards, insects, and even young rattlesnakes for food. Its great speed in running along the ground serves to make this possible.

Some people make a pet of the ground cuckoo. It can be trained to catch mice and other house pests.

You may know this bird by another name. It is also called a road runner.

A Beaver's Home

A beaver's home, called a lodge, always has a flooded lower room. These homes are built in large ponds or streams. Mud and sticks are the main building materials. One room is built above the water level and another room is located under water. The only way a beaver can get into the house is to submerge and enter through an opening in the flooded room. This room serves two purposes: a storage area and a sanctuary from enemies.

Occasionally the lower room becomes dry because the beaver's dam has been destroyed. This energetic animal has to repair the dam quickly or begin building a new home in another place.

The Wildest Run in the World

The Van Hoevenberg bobsled run near Lake Placid, New York, is the wildest bobsled run in the world. This bobsled run is steep, icy, and extremely dangerous. It is almost a mile long and has sixteen sharp curves. High banked walls keep the bobsleds from hurtling off the bobsled run.

Bobsleds used in competitive races are carefully designed. The lead person must be a skillful driver and the back person serves as the brakeperson.

Most championship races at Lake Placid use four-person sleds. The riders bob back and forth together to make the sled go faster. That's how bobsleds got their name. Championship teams at Lake Placid have reached speeds in excess of ninety miles per hour.

Bobsledding has been an Olympic sport since 1924.

So Throw the Ball

One day when my wife turned on our television set to a Yankee-White Sox game, I noticed a phenomenon that intrigued me greatly. I happened to have the *New York Times* on my lap. When the catcher threw the ball back to the White Sox pitcher, I discovered that I could safely look away from the television screen, read a couple of paragraphs in the *Times,* and still revert my eyes in time for the pitch.

Subsequently, I have begun timing baseball games with a stopwatch. I can only conclude that the modern pitcher hates to pitch. He cannot bear the thought of throwing the ball toward the plate. His ingenuity at postponing the fateful moment is uncanny. In the fastest game I have observed, the pitchers on the two teams held the ball for a total of one hour, eight minutes, and thirty seconds!

SUBSKILLS FORMAT
FORM A: POSTTEST

Inventory Record for Teachers

FORM A: Posttest   Inventory Record

Summary Sheet

Student's Name _____ Grade _____ Age (Chronological) _____
yrs. mos.

Date _____ School _____ Administered by _____

Part 1 Word Lists			Part 2 Graded Paragraphs		
Grade Level	Percent of Words Correct	Word Recognition Errors	SIG WR	Comp	L.C.

Part 1 — Word Lists

Grade Level	Percent of Words Correct
PP	_____
P	_____
1	_____
2	_____
3	_____
4	_____
5	_____
6	_____
7	_____
8	_____

Word Recognition Errors

Consonants
____ consonants
____ blends
____ digraphs
____ endings
____ compounds
____ contractions

Vowels
____ long
____ short
____ long/short oo
____ vowel + r
____ diphthong
____ vowel comb.
____ a + l or w

Syllable
____ visual patterns
____ prefix
____ suffix

Word Recognition reinforcement and Vocabulary development

Part 2 — Graded Paragraphs

	SIG WR	Comp	L.C.
PP			
P			
1			
2			
3			
4			
5			
6			
7			
8			

Estimated Levels

	Grade
Independent	_____
Instructional	_____ (range)
Frustration	_____
Listening Capacity	_____

Comp Errors

____ Factual (F)
____ Inference (I)
____ Vocabulary (V)
____ "Word Caller"
(A student who reads without associating meaning)
____ Poor Memory

Summary of Specific Needs:

FORM A: Posttest   Part 1   Graded Word Lists

PP		P		1		2	
1 in	_____	1 three	_____	1 maybe	_____	1 sound	_____
2 now	_____	2 find	_____	2 pass	_____	2 climb	_____
3 so	_____	3 because	_____	3 out	_____	3 waiting	_____
4 from	_____	4 head	_____	4 they	_____	4 hands	_____
5 get	_____	5 their	_____	5 please	_____	5 cry	_____
6 had	_____	6 before	_____	6 love	_____	6 doctor	_____
7 at	_____	7 more	_____	7 cannot	_____	7 people	_____
8 over	_____	8 turn	_____	8 eight	_____	8 everyone	_____
9 of	_____	9 think	_____	9 kind	_____	9 strong	_____
10 into	_____	10 call	_____	10 read	_____	10 inch	_____
11 no	_____	11 these	_____	11 paid	_____	11 rock	_____
12 came	_____	12 school	_____	12 open	_____	12 sea	_____
13 but	_____	13 word	_____	13 top	_____	13 thirty	_____
14 has	_____	14 even	_____	14 pool	_____	14 dance	_____
15 if	_____	15 would	_____	15 low	_____	15 test	_____
16 as	_____	16 ask	_____	16 late	_____	16 hard	_____
17 have	_____	17 much	_____	17 giant	_____	17 dogs	_____
18 be	_____	18 want	_____	18 short	_____	18 story	_____
19 or	_____	19 never	_____	19 upon	_____	19 city	_____
20 an	_____	20 your	_____	20 us	_____	20 push	_____
____%		____%		____%		____%	

Teacher Note: If the child misses five words in any column—stop Part 1. Begin Graded Paragraphs, Part 2 (Form A: Posttest), at the highest level in which the child recognized all twenty words. To save time, if the first ten words were correct, go on to the next list. If one of the words is missed, continue the entire list.

FORM A: Posttest   Part 1   Graded Word Lists

3		4		5		6	
1 computer	_____	1 spy	_____	1 sensation	_____	1 radiant	_____
2 angry	_____	2 downtown	_____	2 analyze	_____	2 greatness	_____
3 energy	_____	3 tray	_____	3 funeral	_____	3 tardy	_____
4 choice	_____	4 lung	_____	4 scissors	_____	4 doughnut	_____
5 hospital	_____	5 exhibit	_____	5 mutual	_____	5 armor	_____
6 court	_____	6 formal	_____	6 consistent	_____	6 nurture	_____
7 heard	_____	7 weekend	_____	7 deliberately	_____	7 dismay	_____
8 closet	_____	8 nineteen	_____	8 officially	_____	8 shipment	_____
9 meet	_____	9 mixture	_____	9 taxi	_____	9 logic	_____
10 picnic	_____	10 invitation	_____	10 parachute	_____	10 pulley	_____
11 against	_____	11 happiness	_____	11 radar	_____	11 fingerprint	_____
12 law	_____	12 gulf	_____	12 intermediate	_____	12 jumbo	_____
13 build	_____	13 rumble	_____	13 embarrass	_____	13 guppy	_____
14 objects	_____	14 plot	_____	14 raid	_____	14 narrator	_____
15 probably	_____	15 tennis	_____	15 crude	_____	15 crutch	_____
16 shot	_____	16 weary	_____	16 bakery	_____	16 shopper	_____
17 we'll	_____	17 lantern	_____	17 knelt	_____	17 punish	_____
18 paragraph	_____	18 preparation	_____	18 endure	_____	18 silken	_____
19 telephone	_____	19 weep	_____	19 painful	_____	19 omelet	_____
20 sugar	_____	20 jelly	_____	20 squash	_____	20 miniature	_____
	_____ %		_____ %		_____ %		_____ %

Teacher Note: If the child misses five words in any column—stop Part 1. Begin Graded Paragraphs, Part 2 (Form A: Posttest), at the highest level in which the child recognized all twenty words. To save time, if the first ten words were correct, go on to the next list. If one of the words is missed, continue the entire list.

FORM A: Posttest   Part 1   Graded Word Lists

7

1 noisily	_____
2 imperative	_____
3 forge	_____
4 expressway	_____
5 nominate	_____
6 include	_____
7 formulate	_____
8 enact	_____
9 depot	_____
10 illegal	_____
11 distress	_____
12 childish	_____
13 unfair	_____
14 sentimental	_____
15 designer	_____
16 luggage	_____
17 historically	_____
18 uncertainty	_____
19 gardener	_____
20 enchant	_____
	_____ %

8.

1 duly	_____
2 furnishing	_____
3 emptiness	_____
4 frustration	_____
5 joyously	_____
6 patriotic	_____
7 zeal	_____
8 seriousness	_____
9 notorious	_____
10 federation	_____
11 youth	_____
12 selection	_____
13 bleak	_____
14 mutton	_____
15 habitation	_____
16 fling	_____
17 dungeon	_____
18 hierarchy	_____
19 duration	_____
20 journalist	_____
	_____ %

Teacher Note: If the child misses five words in any column—stop Part 1. Begin Graded Paragraphs, Part 2 (Form A: Posttest), at the highest level in which the child recognized all twenty words. To save time, if the first ten words were correct, go on to the next list. If one of the words is missed, continue the entire list.

FORM A: Posttest   Part 2/Level PP (24 Words)

Background Knowledge Assessment: This story is about work cars at the airport. Have you ever seen these work cars?

adequate ☐   inadequate ☐

The Work Car

"Look over there," said Jane.

"See the funny little car.

Can you see it?"

"I see it," said Bob.

"It is a work car."

Scoring Guide   Preprimer

SIG WR Errors		**COMP Errors**	
IND	0	IND	0–1
INST	1–2	INST	1½–2
FRUST	3+	FRUST	2½+

Comprehension Check

(F) 1. ____ Who were the children in the story?
(Bob and Jane)

(F) 2. ____ What did they see?
(Funny little car)

(I) 3. ____ Who saw the car first?
(Jane)

(F) 4. ____ What was the car called?
(Work car or help car)

(I) 5. ____ These little work cars go between the planes and the terminal building; what do they do?
(Carry baggage or luggage)

FORM A: Posttest   Part 2/Level P (33 Words)

Background Knowledge Assessment: Have you ever flown on an airplane? Tell me about it. If not, what might it be like?

adequate ☐   inadequate ☐

Jack's First Airplane Ride

Jack and his father got on an airplane.

Away they flew.

"We are up high," said Jack.

"The trees look small."

"And so do the houses," said Father.

Jack said, "This is fun!"

Scoring Guide   Primer

SIG WR Errors		**COMP Errors**	
IND	0	IND	0–1
INST	1–2	INST	1½–2
FRUST	3+	FRUST	2½+

Comprehension Check

(F) 1. ____ Who was with Jack on the airplane?
(Father)

(F) 2. ____ What words in the story told that Jack liked his ride?
(This is fun!)

(V) 3. ____ What did the word "high" mean in the story?
(Way up in the air, above the buildings, trees, etc.)

(I) 4. ____ What in the story told you that Jack and his father were up high?
(The trees and houses looked small. They were flying.)

(F) 5. ____ How many airplane rides did Jack have before this one?
(None)

FORM A: Posttest Part 2/Level 1 (43 Words)

Background Knowledge Assessment: This story is about spiders. What can you tell me about spiders?

adequate ☐   inadequate ☐

Plant Spiders

There are all kinds of spiders.

This black and green one is called a plant spider.

A plant spider has small feet.

All spiders have small feet.

Plant spiders live in nests.

They soon learn to hunt for food and build new nests.

Scoring Guide   First

SIG WR Errors		COMP Errors	
IND	0	IND	0–1
INST	2	INST	1½ –2
FRUST	4+	FRUST	2½+

Comprehension Check

(F) 1. _____ Is there more than one kind of spider?
(Yes—many more)

(F) 2. _____ What two things do plant spiders quickly learn?
(Hunt for food and build new nests)

(F) 3. _____ What color was the spider in this story?
(Black and green)

(F) 4. _____ What did the story say about the spider's feet?
(Small feet, little)

(I) 5. _____ What does this spider probably eat?
(Insects, bugs)

FORM A: Posttest   Part 2/Level 2 (55 Words)

Background Knowledge Assessment: At a rodeo cowboys show their skill with wild horses and bulls. Have you ever seen a rodeo (real, movie, T.V.)?

adequate ☐   inadequate ☐

The Rodeo

The people at the rodeo stood up.

They were all waiting for the big ride.

Everyone came to see Bob Hill ride Midnight.

Bob Hill is a top rider.

Midnight is the best horse in the rodeo.

He is big and fast. Midnight is a strong black horse.

Can Bob Hill ride this great horse?

Comprehension Check

(F) 1. _____ What did the people do?
(Stood up, were waiting, etc.)

(I) 2. _____ The people seemed to be excited. Why?
(They wanted to see this great horse and/or rider.)

(F) 3. _____ What was the name of the horse?
(Midnight)

(F) 4. _____ What did he (Midnight) look like?
(Big, black, strong, etc.)

(F) 5. _____ Why do you think that Bob Hill was a good rider?
(The story said he was a top rider. He had practice.)

Scoring Guide   Second

SIG WR Errors		**COMP Errors**	
IND	0	IND	0–1
INST	3	INST	1½ –2
FRUST	5⁺	FRUST	2½⁺

FORM A: Posttest   Part 2/Level 3 (97 Words)

Background Knowledge Assessment: Baby turkeys do unusual things. What unusual things do you think they do?

adequate ☐   inadequate ☐

Silly Birds

Even with food all around, baby turkeys will not eat. Turkeys can really be called "silly birds." Many die from lack of food. Straw is kept in their houses but some never seem to discover what it is used for. We will never understand senseless turkeys.

The silly young birds don't know enough to come out of the cold, either. So many get sick and die. If they see anything bright, they try to eat it. It may be a pencil, a small nail, or even a shovel. You can see how foolish these "silly birds" are.

Comprehension Check

(F) 1. _____ This story tells about young or old turkeys?
(Young)

(F) 2. _____ What do turkeys do when they see something bright?
(Try to eat it)

(I) 3. _____ What happens to turkeys that do silly things?
(They die)

(F) 4. _____ Tell at least two things that a baby turkey will try to eat.
(Pencil, nail, shovel, or something bright)

(I) 5. _____ What do you think was the most important thing this story told you about turkeys?
(They are very foolish, silly, or dumb)

Scoring Guide   Third

SIG WR Errors		COMP Errors	
IND	2	IND	0–1
INST	5	INST	1½–2
FRUST	10	FRUST	2½+

FORM A: Posttest   Part 2/Level 4 (100 Words)

Background Knowledge Assessment: An exciting sport is called sky diving. Have you ever seen a sky diver in action (T.V., movies)? Tell me about sky diving.

adequate ☐   inadequate ☐

Sky Diving

An exciting sport is sky diving. Sky divers do tricks, make falls, and take interesting pictures. This sport takes you away from your everyday life into a wonderful world you have never known. It is almost like being in a dream. Once out of the airplane, you feel as if you can climb walls or float over mountains.

Sky divers work to develop each of their jumps. Men and women are interested in sky diving. In fact, more people are learning to sky dive each year. This relaxing sport is one of people's adventures.

Comprehension Check

(F) 1. _____ Tell two things that sky divers do.
(Tricks, make falls, take pictures)

(F) 2. _____ Why is sky diving like being in a dream?
(You float, weightlessness, falling, etc.)

(F) 3. _____ Why would people who have a hard week at their job like this sport?
(Relaxing, new world, away from everyday life.)

(I) 4. _____ Why do sky divers need to use airplanes?
(To jump from them.)

(V) 5. _____ Sky divers "work to develop each jump." What does the word "work" mean in this story?
(Do it many times, practices, learn more about it, improves, etc.)

Scoring Guide   Fourth

SIG WR Errors		COMP Errors	
IND	1–2	IND	0–1
INST	5	INST	1½–2
FRUST	9+	FRUST	2½+

FORM A: Posttest   Part 2/Level 5 (104 Words)

Background Knowledge Assessment: When you read this story you will learn that the name ground cuckoo is a special name for a popular bird. What things can you tell about birds?

adequate ☐   inadequate ☐

The Ground Cuckoo

The ground cuckoo is an unusual bird. It is about twenty-four inches long, including its long tail. It also has a long beak and a crested head. You can find it in the southwestern states.

This bird is helpful to people in many ways. It catches small lizards, insects, and even young rattlesnakes for food. Its great speed in running along the ground serves to make this possible.

Some people make a pet of the ground cuckoo. It can be trained to catch mice and other house pests.

You may know this bird by another name. It is also called a road runner.

Comprehension Check

(F) 1. _____ How is the ground cuckoo helpful to people?
(Catches insects, pests, snakes, etc.)

(F) 2. _____ Where is the ground cuckoo found?
(In southwestern United States)

(I) 3. _____ What is unusual about the ground cuckoo?
(Speed, funny looking, etc.)

(F) 4. _____ Describe the ground cuckoo.
(Twenty-four inches long, crested head, long beak, fast runner, etc.)

(F) 5. _____ What is another name for the ground cuckoo?
(Road runner)

Scoring Guide   Fifth

SIG WR Errors		**COMP Errors**	
IND	2	IND	0–1
INST	5	INST	1½–2
FRUST	10	FRUST	2½+

FORM A: Posttest   Part 2/Level 6 (110 Words)

Background Knowledge Assessment: If you have ever been to a zoo you probably saw beavers. Beavers build interesting homes. What can you tell me about a beaver's home or about beavers?

adequate ☐   inadequate ☐

A Beaver's Home

A beaver's home, called a lodge, always has a flooded lower room. These homes are built in large ponds or streams. Mud and sticks are the main building materials. One room is built above the water level and another room is located under water. The only way a beaver can get into the house is to submerge and enter through an opening in the flooded room. This room serves two purposes: a storage area and a sanctuary from enemies.

Occasionally the lower room becomes dry because the beaver's dam has been destroyed. This energetic animal has to repair the dam quickly or begin building a new home in another place.

Comprehension Check

(F) 1. _____ What is the name of a beaver's home?
(Lodge)

(F) 2. _____ Where do beavers build their homes?
(Ponds or streams)

(V) 3. _____ What does the word "submerge" mean?
(Go under water, duck under, dive, etc.)

(I) 4. _____ What would happen to a beaver if there wasn't water in a stream?
(Home would dry up, couldn't live, etc.)

(F) 5. _____ How does a flooded lower room help a beaver?
(Storehouse, escape from enemies, helps him get into house)

Scoring Guide   Sixth

SIG WR Errors		**COMP Errors**	
IND	2	IND	0–1
INST	5-6	INST	1½ –2
FRUST	11	FRUST	2½⁺

FORM A: Posttest   Part 2/Level 7 (126 Words)

Background Knowledge Assessment: Bobsledders race down steep, icy mountain slopes. Bobsledding is an Olympic sport. Can you tell me things about bobsledding?

adequate ☐   inadequate ☐

The Wildest Run in the World

    The Van Hoevenberg bobsled run near Lake Placid, New York, is the wildest bobsled run in the world. This bobsled run is steep, icy, and extremely dangerous. It is almost a mile long and has sixteen sharp curves. High banked walls keep the bobsleds from hurtling off the bobsled run.

    Bobsleds used in competitive races are carefully designed. The lead person must be a skillful driver and the back person serves as the brakeperson.

    Most championship races at Lake Placid use four-person sleds. The riders bob back and forth together to make the sled go faster. That's how bobsleds got their name. Championship teams at Lake Placid have reached speeds in excess of ninety miles per hour.

    Bobsledding has been an Olympic sport since 1924.

Comprehension Check

(F) 1. _____ How many sharp curves did the bobsled run in the story have?
(Sixteen)

(F) 2. _____ What do you call the person on back of the bobsled?
(Brakeperson)

(I) 3. _____ What does the lead person do?
(Steers, drives the sled)

(F) 4. _____ According to the story, how did bobsleds get their name?
(The riders bob back and forth together.)

(V) 5. _____ What does "hurtling" mean?
(Crash, collide, dash violently)

Scoring Guide   Seventh

SIG WR Errors		COMP Errors	
IND	2	IND	0–1
INST	6	INST	1½ –2
FRUST	12	FRUST	2½+

FORM A: Posttest   Part 2/Level 8 (148 Words)

Background Knowledge Assessment: The author has a specific attitude regarding baseball pitchers. Can you guess about the author's attitude?

adequate ☐   inadequate ☐

So Throw the Ball

One day when my wife turned on our television set to a Yankee-White Sox game, I noticed a phenomenon that intrigued me greatly. I happened to have the *New York Times* on my lap. When the catcher threw the ball back to the White Sox pitcher, I discovered that I could safely look away from the television screen, read a couple of paragraphs in the *Times,* and still revert my eyes in time for the pitch.

Subsequently, I have begun timing baseball games with a stopwatch. I can only conclude that the modern pitcher hates to pitch. He cannot bear the thought of throwing the ball toward the plate. His ingenuity at postponing the fateful moment is uncanny. In the fastest game I have observed, the pitchers on the two teams held the ball for a total of one hour, eight minutes, and thirty seconds!

Comprehension Check

(F) 1. _____ Name the teams mentioned in the story.
(Yankees and White Sox)

(F) 2. _____ What paper was the man reading?
(New York Times)

(I) 3. _____ How did the author feel about the pitcher holding the ball so long?
(He felt it was unnecessary.)

(V) 4. _____ What does "ingenuity" mean?
(Clever, original, smart, etc.)

(V) 5. _____ What does "revert" mean?
(To go back, return, etc.)

Scoring Guide   Eighth

SIG WR Errors		COMP Errors	
IND	3	IND	0–1
INST	7–8	INST	1½ –2
FRUST	15	FRUST	2½⁺

SPECIFIC INSTRUCTIONS

For Administering the Reader Response Format
Form B: Pretest and Form B: Posttest

Introduction

The READER RESPONSE FORMAT is based on the following five assumptions. First, the essential factors involved in *reading comprehension* are prior knowledge and prior experience. Second, individual reader responses are affected by the reader's prior knowledge and experience. Third, the reader uses language (reader responses) to organize and reconstruct his or her prior knowledge and experience. Fourth, the reader is able to express prior knowledge and experience by making predictions and retelling the story, in his or her own words. And, finally, it is believed that it is possible to assess the reader's ability to predict and retell and thereby gain valuable insights into the reader's ability to comprehend story material.

Thus, Form B: The Reader Response Format, is designed around the predicting and retelling of stories and divides these two essential factors into the following four scorable parts:

Student Ability	**Scorable Parts**
Predicting	1. *Predicting*—the use of pictures and a title to anticipate story or selection contents.
Retelling	2. *Character(s)*—the use of character(s) to deal with essential elements.
	3. *Problem(s)*—those elements used by the character(s), in the story, to identify problem(s) or reach goal(s).
	4. *Outcome(s)*—usually deals with how the character(s) solved the problem(s) or attained the goal(s).

Prompting and Comfortable Reading Level

Prompting

In order to help assess a student's reading ability, teachers must become familiar with the concept of prompting. Teachers need to know how to prompt, when to prompt, and how much to prompt.

EXAMPLE: Let's say you ask a student to define the word *hat*. The answer you are looking for is: "A hat is something you wear on your head." The student's reply, however, is "A hat is something you wear." This is not a complete answer so you prompt in a *general* way so as not to suggest the answer you want. You say to the student: "Tell me more about a hat." The student replies: "A hat is made of cloth." Still not the answer you are after. Now you prompt in a more *suggestive* way by saying: "Where do you wear a hat?" The student answers, "You wear a hat when you go outside." At this point the prompt becomes *specific* and you say: "Yes, but on what part of your body do you wear a hat?" How much prompting does it take to arrive at the answer you deem necessary to indicate understanding on the student's part?

There are times when the teacher will guide the student by prompting. There are times when prompting is not necessary, and the teacher will not interrupt the free-flow of reader response.

Comfortable Reading Level

What is a comfortable reading level? As the teacher listens to the student read and later discuss the story, is the student an above average, average, or below average reader at a given grade level? If the student, in the teacher's judgment, is reading above average at a given grade level, that is the student's Comfortable Reading Level. STOP! What is meant by above average, average, and below average?

- *Above Average* is synonymous with a student's Independent Reading Level. The oral reading of the story is fluent and expressive; there are few if any significant Word Recognition Errors. During the retelling the student has no difficulty in recalling the character(s), the problem(s), and the outcome(s)/solution(s). This is the student's Comfortable Reading Level.
- *Average* is synonymous with a student's Instructional Reading Level. The oral reading of the selection is somewhat hesitant with an attempt at fluency; there are indications of an increasing number of significant Word Recognition Errors. During the retelling the student exhibits some difficulty in recalling the character(s) or the problem(s) and outcome(s)/solution(s). The teacher found it necessary to do some *general* prompting.
- *Below Average* is synonymous with the student's Frustration Level. The oral reading of the story is word-by-word and with much hesitation; there are a significant number of Word Recognition Errors. During the retelling, even with *suggestive* and *specific* prompting, the student is not able to tell you much about the story.

Preparing Students for Individual Evaluation

Traditionally, reading instruction has required students to read a selection and then to answer questions as a way of developing and assessing comprehension. It seems reasonable to assume that the ability to make predictions and retell the story are usually not taught in most traditional reading programs. If this is true, and the students are in a traditional reading program, the teacher should either; (a) use Form A: Subskills Format or (b) teach students how to predict and retell before administering Form B: Reader Response Format.

In most reading programs, reading evaluation tends to occur near the beginning of the school year. Therefore, it is recommended that before administering Form B: Reader Responses Pre- and Posttests the teacher needs to model the predicting and retelling procedure with the whole class or with small groups.

What follows is a discussion of how to prepare students to make predictions and to retell stories in their own words. This will be followed by an example of how the teacher might actually model the procedure for students. After the discussion and illustration of how to model the procedure for students, the teacher will be able to use Form B: Reader Response Pre- and Posttesting for individual students.

Classroom Environment for Predicting and Retelling

Some students may not become involved easily in making predictions and retelling stories, even after the teacher models the procedure. If students are not sure of what to say or do, teachers may need to base their lessons on student experiences and social activities. The teacher should emphasize that a student's willingness to try is of utmost importance.

The teacher should consider the following:

- Develop themes or topics based on the age and interests of students; for example, young students: animals or pets; older students: T.V. shows.
- Use a variety of instructional groupings: small groups, whole class, or pairs.
- During this preparation period students will need similar copies of stories and titles. Pictures might be included in the copy or placed on the chalkboard.
- During the predicting part, have students use only the title and picture.

Steps in Predicting and Retelling Preparation Period

Predicting: (Allow approximately five minutes for predicting.)

Step 1   Use the title and picture and ask the students to predict the plot or problem. Initially, ask them to work in pairs. Each pair of students can elect to write or discuss their responses. If they do write their responses, do not collect the papers.

Step 2   Ask the students to report their predictions. Record the predictions on the chalkboard, and discuss them. Predictions might be about plot, problems, or words in the title. Tell students they will come back to their predictions after they have had an opportunity to hear the selection read by the teacher and have read it themselves.

Retelling: (Allow approximately ten minutes for retelling.)

Step 3   The students are to follow the selection as the teacher reads it aloud. After the teacher completes the selection, s/he should ask the students to read the selection silently. Again, it is more important for the student to understand the selection than it is for the student to memorize the selection.

Step 4   Go back to step one, and discuss the various student predictions, not on the basis of correct or incorrect (good or bad) responses but rather on how "close" the predictions were or the "fun" of making predictions.

The previous steps merely outline the procedures used during prediction and retelling. What follows is an example of how to introduce these procedures in a lesson where the teacher is asked to model them for students.

Teacher as Model

Find a simple selection. The selection should have a picture and a title. The picture could be a drawing on the chalkboard or an actual picture. The title must be large enough to be seen by the students.

Show the picture and title. The teacher might make several predictions about what s/he thinks the story or selection will be about. Thus the teacher is modeling what the students are expected to do later.

Here is an example of a simple second grade selection:

Find a picture of a bean seed (picture file or encyclopedia)

Title: *From Little Seed to Big Plants*

Predicting: Teacher—"I think that this story is a real or true story. The picture shows a bean seed, and I know that seeds grow into plants. The story might be about how seeds grow into plants. That is my prediction or guess."

Selection: (teacher reads aloud to the students)
"What is in a seed?" asked Betty.
Betty's brother gave her a big bean and said, "Cut this open and see."
Betty cut the bean open. She found a baby plant in the bean.
Betty asked her brother if another bean seed would grow if she planted it.
Betty planted the seed and watered it every day.
When Betty saw the leaves on the plant, she wanted to show them to everyone.

Retelling: Teacher—"The main characters are Betty and her older brother. I think Betty was about seven-years-old. Her brother might have been in high school. (*Problem*) Betty wanted to know what was in a seed. This led Betty to actually grow the seed. I think Betty's brother helped her learn about seeds and how they grow. (*Outcome*) Betty saw the little plant in the seed. After she grew the seed, she learned that seeds grow into plants. I know that Betty was proud of her plant because she wanted to show everybody her new bean plant."

Note: The teacher never asked the students to predict or retell any part of the title or selection. The teacher did everything possible to model the procedure for the students.

The previous procedure is one way to prepare students for Form B: Reader Response Evaluation.

Summary of Specific Instructions—Form B: Reader Response Format

Step 1 The teacher needs to determine if the student understands the story/selection.

Step 2 If the student appears to have the ability to predict and retell the story, do not interrupt with prompting. Strive for a free-flow of information.

Step 3 The questions used in the story guide at each grade level are merely suggestions. Feel free to modify or rephrase them.

Step 4 Take notes or use key words when the student is predicting and retelling on the Inventory Record Form.

Step 5 The teacher may like to tape record the student's responses to review the student's retelling at a later time.

Step 6 Once you become proficient in your ability to hear, prompt, and score retellings, you may not always need to use the tape recorder. However, even when you become proficient, you may want to check your skills occasionally by using the tape recorder.

C R I   I N T E R P R E T A T I O N

Form B: Pretest and Form B: Posttest

The following is a sample CRI record. This example is designed to enable the teacher to gain information on the scoring and interpretation of the Classroom Reading Inventory-Reader Response Format. The sample contains the following:

- A dialogue for *getting started* with a student.
- Examples for scoring a student's responses.
- A sample Inventory Record-Reader Response Format for a second grader—Joan.
- A sample Inventory Record-Summary Sheet for Joan to illustrate how to use and interpret Form B: Reader Response Format.

Getting Started Dialogue

Silvaroli:	"Joan, if I use words like predict or prediction, do you know what I mean?"
Joan:	"No."
Silvaroli:	"How about words like guess or making guesses?"
Joan:	"Yes, because I know how to guess."
Silvaroli:	"O.K., Let's practice making a guess. What do you think the cafeteria is having for lunch today?"
Joan:	"I don't know."
Silvaroli:	"O.K., but you said you knew how to guess. How about making a guess? You don't have to be right. All you need to do is make a guess."
Joan:	"I think they are having hamburgers."
Silvaroli:	"How will you actually know if they are having hamburgers?"
Joan:	"When I go to lunch."
Silvaroli:	"Joan, you made a good guess. Let's make more guesses now. I'm going to show you a picture and the title of a story, and I would like you to make guesses about what the story might be about."

Note: Since Joan is a second grader, the second level selection: *Fish for Sale,* was selected as a place to start the testing.

Scoring a Student's Responses

The Inventory Record for Teachers directs the teacher to score student responses in the areas of Prediction: Picture and Title; Retelling: Character(s), Problem(s), and Outcome(s), on a scale of 1 - 2 - 3. On this scale a score of 1 is low, a score of 2 is average, and a score of 3 is high.

Using Prediction as an example, the teacher would score the student as a 3 (high) if the student was able to predict the story content without any prompting. The teacher would score the student as a 2 (average) if the student was able to predict the story content with only some *general* prompting. The teacher would score the student as a 1 (low) if the student needed *suggestive* and *specific* prompting.

For the areas of Prediction: Picture and Title; Retelling: Character(s), Problem(s), and Outcome(s), the total scoring will be as follows:

TOTAL SCORE

10–12	comprehension excellent
6 – 9	comprehension needs assistance
5 or less	comprehension inadequate

FORM B: Pretest   Inventory Record _____

Summary Sheet

Student's Name _____ Joan _____ Grade __2__ Age (Chronological) __7—4__
yrs. mos.

Date __5/11/96__ School __Troost__ Administered by __N. Silvaroli__

| Level | Predicting-Retelling | | | | | Comfortable Reading Level | | |
	Prediction	Character(s)	Problem(s)	Outcome(s) Solution(s)	TOTAL	Above	Avg.	Below
1.								
2.	3	3	3	3	12	√		
3.	3	1	1	1	6		√	
4.								
5.								
6.								
7.								
8.								

Summary of Responses:

Ability to Predict: _Joan understands and is willing to make predictions_

Ability to Retell: _At the 2nd level, she appears to comprehend the selection._
However, at the 3rd level she needed help with characters, problems and outcomes.

Prompting to Obtain Predicting and Retelling Responses: _considerable_
prompting was needed at the 3rd level.

Comfortable Reading Level: _Joan seems comfortable with 2nd level material._

Comments: _Joan needs specific retelling practice. She appears to be a good_
reader for her age and grade level.

FORM B: Pretest   Level 2

Fish for Sale

Susan got ten fish and a tank for her birthday. She loved the fish and learned to take good care of them.

One day Susan saw six new baby fish in the tank. The fish tank was too small for all of the fish. Dad said he would buy another tank for the baby fish.

Everyone began giving Susan fish and equipment. Soon she had tanks for big fish, small fish, and baby fish.

Each tank had water plants, air tubes, and stones on the bottom.

Mom said, "Enough! Susan, your room looks like a store for fish."

That gave Susan an idea. Why not put all of the fish tanks in the garage and put up a sign?

Susan and her Dad moved everything into the garage.

Susan made a big sign that read, "FISH FOR SALE."

PREDICTION:
Picture and Title   1   2   ③
What do you think is meant by the title, "Fish for Sale?"
What do you think the story will be about?

A kid wanted to buy a fish

The fish are on sale.

_____

RETELLING:
Character(s)   1   2   ③
What do you remember about the people in the story?

Susan got a fish for her birthday. The fish

had baby fish-six I think the story said.

_____

Problem(s)   1   2   ③
What was the problem? What would you do if you had this problem?

Too many fish. Susan needed more tanks.

Susan's mother was upset. The room was

messy. I'd keep the room clean.

Outcome(s)/Solution(s)   1   2   ③
How was the problem solved? What do you think Susan's goal was?

Susan and her Dad moved the fish tanks

to the garage. Susan got the idea to make a

sign and sell the fish.

SCORING GUIDE

TOTAL SCORE ___12___		Prompting		Comfortable Reading Level	
(10–12)	Comprehension excellent	None	✓		
6–9	Comprehension needs assistance	General	___	Above	✓
5 or less	Comprehension inadequate	Specific	___	Average	___
		Suggestive	___	Below	___

FORM B: Pretest   Level 3

The Fox—A Farmer's Friend

"Meg, look! That's a female fox ready to have cubs." Uncle Mike was excited, "I haven't seen a fox around here for ten years." Meg said, "Shall I get your gun?" "There's no need for a gun," Uncle Mike replied. "Foxes help farmers by eating pests like mice, squirrels, frogs, and insects."

The next day Meg and her uncle were unhappy to learn that some farmers were hunting for the fox. These farmers didn't believe that a fox was helpful. Foxes save the farmers' crops by eating pests that destroy their crops. The farmers were sure that foxes only killed chickens and other small animals.

After weeks of hunting, the farmers gave up trying to kill the fox. When Uncle Mike and Meg found fresh fox and cub tracks on the far end of their farm, they were pleased the fox had not been killed.

Student Responses

Low - High   (Circle number)
1   2   3

PREDICTION:

Picture and Title   1   2   ③

Have you ever seen a fox? If no, discuss things about a fox. What do you think the story will be about?

A fox wandered around the woods. It went to this farm house. The farmer keep the fox for a "watch dog."

RETELLING:

Character(s)   ①   2   3

What can you tell me about the people in the story?

Uncle Mike was a good man. The kid . . . I can't remember his name . . . was nice —can't remember anymore.

Problem(s)   ①   2   3

The fox had a problem. What do you think was happening? Why do you think Meg and Uncle Mike worried?

Hunters wanted to kill the fox. (Why did they want to kill the fox?) I don't know. (Why were the kid and uncle Mike worried?) I don't know.

Outcome(s)/Solution(s)   ①   2   3

What happened to the fox? When Uncle Mike and Meg saw the tracks, what did they learn? How did Uncle Mike and Meg feel?

The fox didn't get killed. (How do you know that the fox didn't get killed?) I guessed— that's all I know.

SCORING GUIDE

TOTAL SCORE ___6___

		Comfortable Reading Level
10–12 Comprehension excellent	**Prompting**	
⑥–9 Comprehension needs assistance	None _____	
5 or less Comprehension inadequate	General _____	Above _____
	Specific _✓_	Average _____
	Suggestive _✓_	Below _✓_

Summary of Specific Instructions

Step 1   Establish rapport. Don't be in a hurry to begin testing. Put the student at ease. Make him/her feel comfortable.

Step 2   Begin at the level of the student's current grade level. If, for example, the student is a third grader, begin with a third grade selection. If the student has the ability to predict and retell and is reading comfortably, go to the fourth grade level selection. If the student is having difficulty, drop back to the second grade level selection. If you have reason to believe that the student is reading above or below grade level, adjust the starting level accordingly.

Step 3   Ask the student to look at the picture as you read the title aloud. Take care to cover the selection while reading. Using the picture and title, ask the student to predict, to make guesses about the selection. If necessary, use prompting.

Step 4   Have the student read the selection aloud to you. After reading, ask the student to retell the story by noting character(s), problem(s), and outcome(s)/solution(s). The guided questions listed for the predicting and retelling scorable areas are merely suggestions. Feel free to change them as needed.

Step 5   If it becomes necessary to prompt, use a *general* prompt first so as to not give the story away. If the student needs *suggestive* or *specific* prompting, it is safe to assume that the student is having difficulty comprehending what s/he is reading.

Step 6   As previously stated, the Comfortable Reading Level is the level at which the student is able to read without difficulty; in other words, the oral reading of the story is fluent and expressive and there are few if any significant word recognition errors. During the retelling the student has no difficulty in recalling the character(s), the problem(s), and the outcome(s)/solution(s).

Step 7   Transfer the Comfortable Reading Level and the scorable parts total to the Inventory Record—Summary Sheet.

READER RESPONSE FORMAT
FORM B: PRETEST

Graded Paragraphs

It's My Ball

Tom and Nancy went for a walk.
They saw a small ball on the grass.
They began fighting over the ball.
While they were fighting, a dog picked up the ball and ran.
The kids ran after the dog, but the dog got away.

Fish for Sale

Susan got ten fish and a tank for her birthday.
She loved the fish and learned to take good care of them.
One day Susan saw six new baby fish in the tank.
The fish tank was too small for all of the fish.
Dad said he would buy another tank for the baby fish.
Everyone began giving Susan fish and equipment.
Soon she had tanks for big fish, small fish, and baby fish.
Each tank had water plants, air tubes, and stones on the bottom.
Mom said, "Enough! Susan, your room looks like a store for fish."
That gave Susan an idea. Why not put all of the fish tanks in the garage and put up a sign?
Susan and her Dad moved everything into the garage.
Susan made a big sign that read, "FISH FOR SALE."

The Fox—A Farmer's Friend

"Meg, look! That's a female fox ready to have cubs." Uncle Mike was excited, "I haven't seen a fox around here for ten years." Meg said, "Shall I get your gun?" "There's no need for a gun," Uncle Mike replied. "Foxes help farmers by eating pests like mice, squirrels, frogs, and insects."

The next day Meg and her uncle were unhappy to learn that some farmers were hunting for the fox. These farmers didn't believe that a fox was helpful. Foxes save the farmers' crops by eating pests that destroy their crops. The farmers were sure that foxes only killed chickens and other small animals.

After weeks of hunting, the farmers gave up trying to kill the fox. When Uncle Mike and Meg found fresh fox and cub tracks on the far end of their farm, they were pleased the fox had not been killed.

Floods Are Dangerous

Mrs. Foley was driving home with her two sons, nine-year-old Peter and eleven-year-old Jason. Lightning flashed, thunder shook the ground, and the rain poured down. In order to get home, Mrs. Foley had to cross a road covered with water. She decided to drive across the rushing water. When the car was about halfway across the road, the water rose higher, and the car began to float away. Mrs. Foley knew that she had to get the boys and herself out of that car.

Eleven-year-old Jason was able to roll down the window and jump to a small hill. Mrs. Foley also jumped to the hill. Mrs. Foley and Jason tried to grab Peter, but the car was pushed downstream.

Soon the police and friends came, and they searched all night for Peter. Peter was nowhere to be seen. Had Peter drowned in the flood, or was he safe?

Early the next day Mrs. Foley heard horns blowing and neighbors shouting, "Peter is safe." Peter told everyone how he got out of the car but then he got lost in the dark. Everyone was happy to see Peter again.

The Great Railroad

President Lincoln had a dream for the future. He wanted a railroad built between Nebraska and California. In 1862, Mr. Lincoln's dream began to come true when he signed the Pacific Railroad Act. Soon after, he employed Mr. Dodge, an engineer, to direct the building of the railroad.

Mr. Dodge decided to build the railroad in two directions. He used one company called the Central Pacific Railroad to work from California eastward. The other was called the Union Pacific Railroad. They worked from Nebraska westward. More than 20,000 workers were soon laying track from east and west.

In this project, costs were high and problems were many. Each company had to transport such things as food, clothing, medicine, and track. The workers had to blast tunnels; build bridges; and cross high, snow-covered mountains.

On May 10, 1869, leaders of both companies drove a golden spike into the final rail. Mr. Dodge, the project director, had tears in his eyes as the two trains touched. He thought about his first meeting with Lincoln. Mr. Dodge was thrilled that the railroad was completed but sad that President Lincoln did not live to see his dream come true.

A Different Kind of Courage

Mike overheard an older guy named Buster bragging that he skied the old abandoned ski trail called **Killer Hill.** Mike, a sixth grader, decided that if Buster could do it so could he. Mike told his parents that he wanted to ski **Killer Hill.**

"You gone off your head Mike?" his father said. "That darn trail could kill you."

Mike knew the risks, and he feared them. While getting ready for bed, he thought maybe he was a fool, but he wouldn't stop now.

While Mike, his parents, and his two best friends were driving to the ski slopes, his father said, "Why do you want to do such a crazy thing?"

Mike thought, how could he explain that he wanted to show up Buster.

Mike's father was saying, "That hill is dangerous. Use the regular trails."

Mike whispered, "Regular trails are for kids."

His father grinned, "Maybe so—but be careful son."

"I will, Pop, I promise."

When they reached the top of the ski lift, Mike headed for **Killer Hill.** He didn't realize it, but his friends and others, including Buster, followed him. Mike was about to push off when his friends yelled, "Mike—don't do it!" This caused him to hesitate.

Buster shouted, "What's the matter—are you chicken?"

Mike's friends were excited and screamed, "Mike, please, please don't do it."

Suddenly he knew they were right; he was trying to show off—just like Buster. Mike turned and joined his friends.

He wished he could tell someone how it was—that it was harder to let Buster think he was yellow than it would have been to ski the trail.

Mike couldn't explain it, but it took a different kind of courage to let himself be ridiculed for something others couldn't understand.

Bar Codes in a Modern Supermarket

When Mike was a teenager, he got a part-time job in a local supermarket marking prices on grocery products. He used a hand-held stamping machine to mark products, such as cans and boxes. Mike worked at the supermarket after school and on weekends for several years.

One day the store manager introduced a new computerized system called the Universal Product Code (UPC). The bar code is printed on a wide variety of products and has eleven digits as well as lines and bars. At the checkout counter, the store clerk passes the code for each product, face down, over a small window. A beam of light "reads" the code and sends the information to the store's computer. With this bar code the store can keep track of each product.

After a short time, Mike was asked to work fewer hours because the bar code was so efficient. Mike decided to go to college to learn about computers. After college, Mike got a job selling computerized bar codes to supermarkets.

Democracy Versus Communism

The practice of government is thousands of years old. Some types of governments have been in use for hundreds of years. The two types of governments used in large major countries are democracy and Communism.

The United States government is over two hundred years old and has a well-developed form of democracy. The United States has a two-house Congress and a constitution that is the supreme law of the land. In the United States the citizens have the individual right to vote for who or what they believe. They also have the right to individually own property and to wealth.

Communism is a form of government that believes that property and wealth should be owned in *common* or *belong to all of the people*. Communism, as a form of government, is about eighty years old.

People in different countries continue to argue over which form of government is best.

Democracy, like Communism, has its strengths and weaknesses. However, more and more countries have adopted democracy as their form of government.

READER RESPONSE FORMAT
FORM B: PRETEST

Inventory Record for Teachers

FORM B: Pretest   Inventory Record

Summary Sheet

Student's Name _____ Grade _____ Age (Chronological) _____
yrs. mos.

Date _____ School _____ Administered by _____

	Predicting-Retelling					Comfortable Reading Level		
Level	Prediction	Character(s)	Problem(s)	Outcome(s) Solution(s)	TOTAL	Above	Avg.	Below
1.								
2.								
3.								
4.								
5.								
6.								
7.								
8.								

Summary of Responses:

Ability to Predict: _____

_____

_____

Ability to Retell: _____

_____

_____

Prompting to Obtain Predicting and Retelling Responses: _____

_____

_____

Comfortable Reading Level: _____

Comments: _____

_____

FORM B: Pretest   Level 1

It's My Ball

Tom and Nancy went for a walk.

They saw a small ball on the grass.

They began fighting over the ball.

While they were fighting, a dog picked

up the ball and ran.

The kids ran after the dog, but the dog

got away.

PREDICTION:
Picture and Title   1   2   3
What do you think the story will be about?

_____

_____

_____

RETELLING:
Character(s)   1   2   3
What do you remember about the people in the story?

_____

_____

Problem(s)   1   2   3
What was the problem? If you were in that situation
what would you do?

_____

_____

Outcome(s)/Solution(s)   1   2   3
How was the problem solved?

_____

_____

_____

SCORING GUIDE

TOTAL SCORE _____		Prompting		Comfortable Reading Level	
10–12	Comprehension excellent	None	_____		
6–9	Comprehension needs assistance	General	_____	Above	_____
5 or less	Comprehension inadequate	Specific	_____	Average	_____
		Suggestive	_____	Below	_____

FORM B: Pretest   Level 2

Fish for Sale

Susan got ten fish and a tank for her birthday. She loved the fish and learned to take good care of them.

One day Susan saw six new baby fish in the tank. The fish tank was too small for all of the fish. Dad said he would buy another tank for the baby fish.

Everyone began giving Susan fish and equipment. Soon she had tanks for big fish, small fish, and baby fish.

Each tank had water plants, air tubes, and stones on the bottom.

Mom said, "Enough! Susan, your room looks like a store for fish."

That gave Susan an idea. Why not put all of the fish tanks in the garage and put up a sign?

Susan and her Dad moved everything into the garage.

Susan made a big sign that read, "FISH FOR SALE."

Low - High   (Circle number)
1   2   3

PREDICTION:
Picture and Title   1   2   3
What do you think is meant by the title, "Fish for Sale"?
What do you think the story will be about?

_____

_____

_____

RETELLING:
Character(s)   1   2   3
What do you remember about the people in the story?

_____

_____

_____

Problem(s)   1   2   3
What was the problem? What would you do if you had this problem?

_____

_____

_____

Outcome(s)/Solution(s)   1   2   3
How was the problem solved? What do you think Susan's goal was?

_____

_____

_____

SCORING GUIDE

TOTAL SCORE _____		Prompting		Comfortable Reading Level	
10–12	Comprehension excellent	None	_____		
6–9	Comprehension needs assistance	General	_____	Above	_____
5 or less	Comprehension inadequate	Specific	_____	Average	_____
		Suggestive	_____	Below	_____

FORM B: Pretest Level 3

The Fox—A Farmer's Friend

"Meg, look! That's a female fox ready to have cubs." Uncle Mike was excited, "I haven't seen a fox around here for ten years." Meg said, "Shall I get your gun?" "There's no need for a gun," Uncle Mike replied. "Foxes help farmers by eating pests like mice, squirrels, frogs, and insects."

The next day Meg and her uncle were unhappy to learn that some farmers were hunting for the fox. These farmers didn't believe that a fox was helpful. Foxes save the farmers' crops by eating pests that destroy their crops. The farmers were sure that foxes only killed chickens and other small animals.

After weeks of hunting, the farmers gave up trying to kill the fox. When Uncle Mike and Meg found fresh fox and cub tracks on the far end of their farm, they were pleased the fox had not been killed.

PREDICTION:
Picture and Title   1   2   3
Have you ever seen a fox? If no, discuss things about a fox. What do you think the story will be about?

_____

_____

_____

RETELLING:
Character(s)   1   2   3
What can you tell me about the people in the story?

_____

_____

_____

Problem(s)   1   2   3
The fox had a problem. What do you think was happening? Why do you think Meg and Uncle Mike worried?

_____

_____

_____

Outcome(s)/Solution(s)   1   2   3
What happened to the fox? When Uncle Mike and Meg saw the tracks, what did they learn? How did Uncle Mike and Meg feel?

_____

_____

_____

SCORING GUIDE

TOTAL SCORE _____		Prompting	Comfortable Reading Level
10–12	Comprehension excellent	None _____	
6–9	Comprehension needs assistance	General _____	Above _____
5 or less	Comprehension inadequate	Specific _____	Average _____
		Suggestive _____	Below _____

FORM B: Pretest   Level 4

Floods Are Dangerous

Mrs. Foley was driving home with her two sons, nine-year-old Peter and eleven-year-old Jason. Lightning flashed, thunder shook the ground, and the rain poured down. In order to get home, Mrs. Foley had to cross a road covered with water. She decided to drive across the rushing water. When the car was about halfway across the road, the water rose higher, and the car began to float away. Mrs. Foley knew that she had to get the boys and herself out of that car.

Eleven-year-old Jason was able to roll down the window and jump to a small hill. Mrs. Foley also jumped to the hill. Mrs. Foley and Jason tried to grab Peter, but the car was pushed downstream.

Soon the police and friends came, and they searched all night for Peter. Peter was nowhere to be seen. Had Peter drowned in the flood, or was he safe?

Early the next day Mrs. Foley heard horns blowing and neighbors shouting, "Peter is safe." Peter told everyone how he got out of the car but then he got lost in the dark. Everyone was happy to see Peter again.

Student Responses

Low - High   (Circle number)
1   2   3

PREDICTION:
Picture and Title   1   2   3
What do you think the story will be about?

_____

_____

_____

RETELLING:
Character(s)   1   2   3
What do you remember about the people in the story? How do you think they felt?

_____

_____

_____

Problem(s)   1   2   3
What was the problem? What do you think caused the problem?

_____

_____

_____

Outcome(s)/Solution(s)   1   2   3
How do you think the problem was solved? How do you think you would feel in this situation?

_____

_____

_____

SCORING GUIDE

TOTAL SCORE _____		Prompting		Comfortable Reading Level	
10–12	Comprehension excellent	None	_____		
6–9	Comprehension needs assistance	General	_____	Above	_____
5 or less	Comprehension inadequate	Specific	_____	Average	_____
		Suggestive	_____	Below	_____

FORM B: Pretest   Level 5

The Great Railroad

President Lincoln had a dream for the future. He wanted a railroad built between Nebraska and California. In 1862, Mr. Lincoln's dream began to come true when he signed the Pacific Railroad Act. Soon after, he employed Mr. Dodge, an engineer, to direct the building of the railroad.

Mr. Dodge decided to build the railroad in two directions. He used one company called the Central Pacific Railroad to work from California eastward. The other was called the Union Pacific Railroad. They worked from Nebraska westward. More than 20,000 workers were soon laying track from east and west.

In this project, costs were high and problems were many. Each company had to transport such things as food, clothing, medicine, and track. The workers had to blast tunnels; build bridges; and cross high, snow-covered mountains.

On May 10, 1869, leaders of both companies drove a golden spike into the final rail. Mr. Dodge, the project director, had tears in his eyes as the two trains touched. He thought about his first meeting with Lincoln. Mr. Dodge was thrilled that the railroad was completed but sad that President Lincoln did not live to see his dream come true.

PREDICTION:
Picture and Title   1   2   3
Tell why you think this was a great railroad.

_____

_____

_____

RETELLING:
Character(s)   1   2   3
In your opinion who was the main person or persons in the story?

_____

_____

_____

Problem(s)   1   2   3
Why do you think Mr. Dodge used two companies? What types of problems did these companies have?

_____

_____

_____

Outcome(s)/Solution(s)   1   2   3
What in your opinion was the goal?

_____

_____

_____

SCORING GUIDE

TOTAL SCORE _____		Prompting		Comfortable Reading Level	
10–12	Comprehension excellent	None	_____		
6–9	Comprehension needs assistance	General	_____	Above	_____
5 or less	Comprehension inadequate	Specific	_____	Average	_____
		Suggestive	_____	Below	_____

FORM B: Pretest   Level 6

A Different Kind of Courage

Mike overheard an older guy named Buster bragging that he skied the old abandoned ski trail called **Killer Hill.** Mike, a sixth grader, decided that if Buster could do it so could he. Mike told his parents that he wanted to ski **Killer Hill.**

"You gone off your head Mike?" his father said. "That darn trail could kill you."

Mike knew the risks, and he feared them. While getting ready for bed, he thought maybe he was a fool, but he wouldn't stop now.

While Mike, his parents, and his two best friends were driving to the ski slopes, his father said, "Why do you want to do such a crazy thing?" Mike thought, how could he explain that he wanted to show up Buster. Mike's father was saying, "That hill is dangerous. Use the regular trails." Mike whispered, "Regular trails are for kids." His father grinned, "Maybe so—but be careful son." "I will, Pop, I promise."

When they reached the top of the ski lift, Mike headed for **Killer Hill.** He didn't realize it, but his friends and others, including Buster, followed him. Mike was about to push off when his friends yelled, "Mike—don't do it!" This caused him to hesitate.

Buster shouted, "What's the matter—are you chicken?" Mike's friends were excited and screamed, "Mike, please, please don't do it." Suddenly he knew they were right; he was trying to show off—just like Buster.

Mike turned and joined his friends. He wished he could tell someone how it was—that it was harder to let Buster think he was yellow than it would have been to ski the trail.

Mike couldn't explain it, but it took a different kind of courage to let himself be ridiculed for something others couldn't understand.

Student Responses

Low - High   (Circle number)
1   2   3

PREDICTION:
Picture and Title   1   2   3
What do you think the title and picture tell you about the story? _____

_____

RETELLING:
Character(s)   1   2   3
What do you remember about the people in the story?

_____

_____

Problem(s)   1   2   3
What was the problem? What do you think is meant by "a different kind of courage"?

_____

_____

Outcome(s)/Solution(s)   1   2   3
How was the problem solved? How did Mike feel? Why do you think Mike had difficulty explaining how he felt? _____

_____

SCORING GUIDE

TOTAL SCORE _____		Prompting		Comfortable Reading Level	
10–12	Comprehension excellent	None	_____		
6–9	Comprehension needs assistance	General	_____	Above	_____
5 or less	Comprehension inadequate	Specific	_____	Average	_____
		Suggestive	_____	Below	_____

FORM B: Pretest   Level 7

Bar Codes in a Modern Supermarket

When Mike was a teenager, he got a part-time job in a local supermarket marking prices on grocery products. He used a hand-held stamping machine to mark products, such as cans and boxes. Mike worked at the supermarket after school and on weekends for several years.

One day the store manager introduced a new computerized system called the Universal Product Code (UPC). The bar code is printed on a wide variety of products and has eleven digits as well as lines and bars. At the checkout counter, the store clerk passes the code for each product, face down, over a small window. A beam of light "reads" the code and sends the information to the store's computer. With this bar code, the store can keep track of each product.

After a short time, Mike was asked to work fewer hours because the bar code was so efficient. Mike decided to go to college to learn about computers. After college, Mike got a job selling computerized bar codes to supermarkets.

Student Responses

Low - High   (Circle number)
1   2   3

PREDICTION:
Picture and Title   1   2   3
What do you think the title and picture tell you about the story?

_____

_____

_____

RETELLING:
Character(s)   1   2   3
Who was the main person in the story?

_____

_____

_____

Problem(s)   1   2   3
What was the problem? Why did Mike have to work fewer hours? What did the bar code have to do with the problem?

_____

_____

_____

Outcome(s)/Solution(s)   1   2   3
What did Mike decide to do?

_____

_____

_____

_____

SCORING GUIDE

TOTAL SCORE _____		Prompting		Comfortable Reading Level	
10–12	Comprehension excellent	None	_____		
6 – 9	Comprehension needs assistance	General	_____	Above	_____
5 or less	Comprehension inadequate	Specific	_____	Average	_____
		Suggestive	_____	Below	_____

FORM B: Pretest   Level 8

Democracy Versus Communism

The practice of government is thousands of years old. Some types of governments have been in use for hundreds of years. The two types of governments used in large major countries are democracy and Communism.

The United States government is over two hundred years old and has a well-developed form of democracy. The United States has a two-house Congress and a constitution that is the supreme law of the land. In the United States the citizens have the individual right to vote for who or what they believe. They also have the right to individually own property and to wealth.

Communism is a form of government that believes that property and wealth should be owned in *common* or *belong to all of the people*. Communism, as a form of government, is about eighty years old. People in different countries continue to argue over which form of government is best.

Democracy, like Communism, has its strengths and weaknesses. However, more and more countries have adopted democracy as their form of government.

PREDICTION:
Picture and Title   1   2   3
The picture and title are not much help in predicting what this story is about. The story is really about an idea. Can you tell me what is meant by government?

_____

_____

_____

RETELLING:
Character(s)   1   2   3
The story tells about two types of governments. Are you able to tell things about these two forms of governments?

_____

_____

_____

Problem(s)/Outcomes   1   2   3
What type of government does the author believe is the better form of government? Tell all you can about democracy and Communism.

_____

_____

_____

SCORING GUIDE

TOTAL SCORE _____		Prompting		Comfortable Reading Level	
10–12	Comprehension excellent	None	_____		
6–9	Comprehension needs assistance	General	_____	Above	_____
5 or less	Comprehension inadequate	Specific	_____	Average	_____
		Suggestive	_____	Below	_____

READER RESPONSE FORMAT
FORM B: POSTTEST

Graded Paragraphs

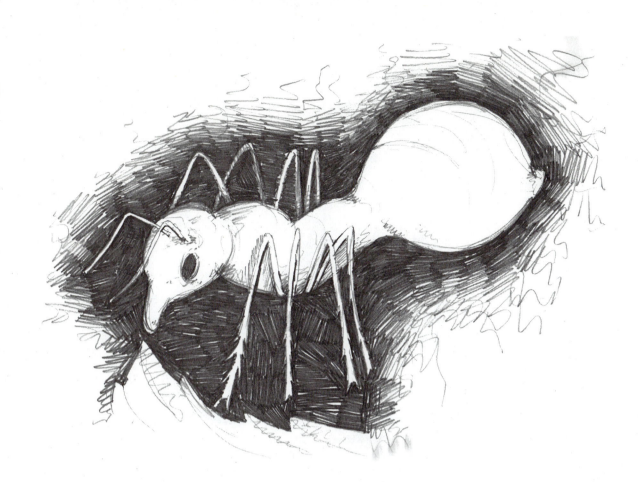

The Red Ant

The red ant lives under the sand.
The ant must build its own room.
It has to take the sand outside.
The sand is made into little hills.
Building a room is hard work.
The red ant is a busy bug.

Why Can't I Play?

Kim wanted to play on the boys' soccer team.

The boys said, "No."

One day the boys needed one more player.

They asked Kim to play.

Kim got the ball and kicked it a long way.

She was a fast runner and a good player.

Todd, a boy on the team, kicked the ball to her.

Kim kicked the ball down the side of the field.

Tony, a boy on the other team, tried to block her.

He missed and Kim scored.

Someone said, "Kim should have played on the team all year."

Smart Birds Know What To Eat

Everyone knows that birds like to eat seeds and grain. Birds also like to eat little stones called gravel. Birds have to eat the gravel because they don't have teeth to grind their food. The gravel stays in the bird's gizzard, which is something like a stomach. When the bird eats seed, the gravel and the seed grind together. All of the seed is mashed up.

Tame birds must be given gravel. Wild birds find their own gravel on the road sides. Now you can see how smart birds are.

Traveling West

A dozen men walked quickly along a forest trail. They were bound for the salt springs near the mountains. Each man led a pack horse. These men were with a wagon train and had never been in this country before. They didn't like to go to the springs now, but they had to have salt. New settlers had been bringing salt, but that was about gone.

At the head of the line walked one of the best guides in the West, young Daniel Boone.

Daniel Boone was prepared for hardships because he had been hunting for two long years.

An Underwater School

A team of scientists proved that seals have a keen sense of hearing. These men and women trained blind seals to expect food when they heard sounds. The seals always began snapping when a shrill signal was sounded.

It was proved that even a soft signal, a considerable distance away, could make these sea mammals respond. That should make the fisher who splashes his/her oars, or talks loudly, start thinking.

The same team of scientists also trained seals to recognize different sounds. One bell-tone meant food, two bell-tones meant no food. In the beginning, the seals made mistakes when the two-bell tones were sounded. They were given a light tap after each mistake. The seals were quick learners. They easily learned to tell the difference between the sounds.

Sentinels in the Forest

Many wild creatures that travel with their own kind know by instinct how to protect the group. One of them acts as a sentinel.

Hidden by the branches of a low-hanging tree, I once watched two white-tailed deer feeding in a meadow. At first, my interest was held by their beauty. Soon I noticed something quite unusual; they were taking turns feeding. While one was calmly cropping grass, unafraid and at ease, the other—with head high, eyes sweeping the sea marsh and sensitive nostrils "feeling" the air—stood on guard against enemies. Not for a moment, during the half hour I spied upon them, did they stop their teamwork.

Danger on the Bike Track

All week, Ed Pike, a young race driver, put his BMX (bicycle moto-cross) racer through a series of test runs. Ed was preparing for the biggest race of the year. He was going to race against another top BMX racer named Jimmy Scott.

The race was to take place on a dangerous track with many bumps and sharp turns. Moto-cross bicycles have small wheels and wide tires to help prevent them from slipping in the turns. Ed knew that he needed something special to beat Jimmy. He decided to use a type of tire never used before.

Jimmy complained that Ed's tires were illegal. The race officials checked the tires and said that Ed was able to use them. Ed Pike felt that he was in real danger because Jimmy was angry about the tires. Soon after the race started, Jimmy tried to cut Ed off but he missed. Ed gave his BMX full power and pulled ahead of Jimmy and the others. Jimmy should have paid attention to his own skill and his bike's performance and not worry about Ed's new tires.

Courage

Courage is the quality people like most and primitive males gauged their manhood by it as do modern adolescents. Civilized people are dazzled by showy courage. An example are the people at Acapulco who dive off a cliff into the sea. Another is the racing car driver or the trapeze artist, or the bystander who runs through flames to save a stranger.

There is a truer courage that is more gallant though almost invisible. It is found in the steadfastness of ordinary people who very matter-of-factly raise children with disabilities. Courage is found in those people who live in never-ending pain and yet do not hate others. It is found in people who, giving up malice and suspicion, teach themselves to relax and trust. It is also found in the quiet acceptance of monotonous jobs that must be done, yet it's the kind of courage people rarely recognize in themselves.

READER RESPONSE FORMAT
FORM B: POSTTEST

Inventory Record for Teachers

FORM B: Posttest   Inventory Record

Summary Sheet

Student's Name _____ Grade _____ Age (Chronological) _____
yrs. mos.

Date _____ School _____ Administered by _____

Level	Predicting-Retelling					Comfortable Reading Level		
	Prediction	Character(s)	Problem(s)	Outcome(s) Solution(s)	TOTAL	Above	Avg.	Below
1.								
2.								
3.								
4.								
5.								
6.								
7.								
8.								

Summary of Responses:

Ability to Predict: _____

_____

_____

Ability to Retell: _____

_____

_____

Prompting to Obtain Predicting and Retelling Responses: _____

_____

_____

Comfortable Reading Level: _____

Comments: _____

_____

FORM B: Posttest　Level 1

The Red Ant

The red ant lives under the sand.

The ant must build its own room.

It has to take the sand outside.

The sand is made into little hills.

Building a room is hard work.

The red ant is a busy bug.

PREDICTION:
Picture and Title　　　1　　2　　3
What do you think the story will be about?

_____

_____

_____

RETELLING:
Character(s)　　　　　　1　　2　　3
What can you tell me about the red ant?

_____

_____

_____

Problem(s)　　　　　　1　　2　　3
What did the red ant have to do to build its room?

_____

_____

_____

Outcome(s)/Solution(s)　　1　　2　　3
What can you tell me about the red ant's work habits?

_____

_____

_____

_____

SCORING GUIDE

TOTAL SCORE _____		Prompting	Comfortable Reading Level
10–12	Comprehension excellent	None _____	
6 – 9	Comprehension needs assistance	General _____	Above _____
5 or less	Comprehension inadequate	Specific _____	Average _____
		Suggestive _____	Below _____

FORM B: Posttest   Level 2

Why Can't I Play?

Kim wanted to play on the boys' soccer team.

The boys said, "No."

One day the boys needed one more player.

They asked Kim to play.

Kim got the ball and kicked it a long way.

She was a fast runner and a good player.

Todd, a boy on the team, kicked the ball to her.

Kim kicked the ball down the side of the field.

Tony, a boy on the other team, tried to block her.

He missed and Kim scored.

Someone said, "Kim should have played on the team all year."

Student Responses

Low - High   (Circle number)
1   2   3

PREDICTION:
Picture and Title   1   2   3
What do you think is meant by the title, "Why Can't I Play?" What do you think the story will be about?

_____

_____

_____

RETELLING:
Character(s)   1   2   3
Who was the main person in the story? Can you tell me more about that person?

_____

_____

_____

Problem(s)   1   2   3
What was the problem? Can you tell me anything more?

_____

_____

_____

Outcome(s)/Solution(s)   1   2   3
How was the problem solved?

_____

_____

_____

SCORING GUIDE

TOTAL SCORE _____		Prompting	Comfortable Reading Level
10–12	Comprehension excellent	None _____	
6 – 9	Comprehension needs assistance	General _____	Above _____
5 or less	Comprehension inadequate	Specific _____	Average _____
		Suggestive _____	Below _____

FORM B: Posttest   Level 3

Smart Birds Know What To Eat

Everyone knows that birds like to eat seeds and grain. Birds also like to eat little stones called gravel. Birds have to eat the gravel because they don't have teeth to grind their food. The gravel stays in the bird's gizzard, which is something like a stomach. When the bird eats seed, the gravel and the seed grind together. All of the seed is mashed up.

Tame birds must be given gravel. Wild birds find their own gravel on the road sides. Now you can see how smart birds are.

Student Responses

Low - High   (Circle number)
1   2   3

PREDICTION:
Picture and Title   1   2   3
Why do you think birds are smart?

_____

_____

_____

RETELLING:
Character(s)   1   2   3
This story is not about people. Can you tell me what the story said about birds?

_____

_____

_____

Problem(s)   1   2   3
What did the story say about birds eating gravel? Why do they have to eat gravel?

_____

_____

_____

Outcome(s)/Solution(s)   1   2   3
Can you tell what happens to birds that do not eat gravel?

_____

_____

_____

SCORING GUIDE

TOTAL SCORE _____		Prompting		Comfortable Reading Level	
10–12	Comprehension excellent	None	_____		
6 – 9	Comprehension needs assistance	General	_____	Above	_____
5 or less	Comprehension inadequate	Specific	_____	Average	_____
		Suggestive	_____	Below	_____

FORM B: Posttest   Level 4

Traveling West

A dozen men walked quickly along a forest trail. They were bound for the salt springs near the mountains. Each man led a pack horse. These men were with a wagon train and had never been in this country before. They didn't like to go to the springs now, but they had to have salt. New settlers had been bringing salt, but that was about gone.

At the head of the line walked one of the best guides in the west, young Daniel Boone.

Daniel Boone was prepared for hardships because he had been hunting for two long years.

Student Responses

Low - High   (Circle number)
1   2   3

PREDICTION:
Picture and Title   1   2   3
What will this story be about? Tell me all you can about the story.

_____

_____

_____

RETELLING:
Character(s)   1   2   3
Of the many men on the trail, who do you think was the main person or leader?

_____

_____

_____

Problem(s)   1   2   3
What were the men looking for? What did the story say about Daniel Boone?

_____

_____

_____

Outcome(s)/Solution(s)   1   2   3
This story didn't have a clear ending. Why?

_____

_____

_____

SCORING GUIDE

TOTAL SCORE _____		Prompting		Comfortable Reading Level	
10–12	Comprehension excellent	None	_____		
6–9	Comprehension needs assistance	General	_____	Above	_____
5 or less	Comprehension inadequate	Specific	_____	Average	_____
		Suggestive	_____	Below	_____

FORM B: Posttest   Level 5

An Underwater School

A team of scientists proved that seals have a keen sense of hearing. These men and women trained blind seals to expect food when they heard sounds. The seals always began snapping when a shrill signal was sounded.

It was proved that even a soft signal, a considerable distance away, could make these sea mammals respond. That should make the fisher who splashes his/her oars, or talks loudly, start thinking.

The same team of scientists also trained seals to recognize different sounds. One bell-tone meant food, two bell-tones meant no food. In the beginning, some of the seals made mistakes when the two-bell tones were sounded. They were given a light tap after each mistake. The seals were quick learners. They easily learned to tell the difference between the sounds.

Student Responses

Low - High   (Circle number)
1   2   3

PREDICTION:
Picture and Title   1   2   3
What will this story be about?

_____

_____

_____

RETELLING:
Character(s)   1   2   3
This story was not about a specific person, it was about a group of people called scientists. Tell me what they were doing.

_____

_____

_____

Problem(s)   1   2   3
What were the scientists trying to prove?

_____

_____

_____

Outcome(s)/Solution(s)   1   2   3
Tell some things that the seals learned.

_____

_____

SCORING GUIDE

TOTAL SCORE _____		Prompting	Comfortable Reading Level
10–12	Comprehension excellent	None _____	
6–9	Comprehension needs assistance	General _____	Above _____
5 or less	Comprehension inadequate	Specific _____	Average _____
		Suggestive _____	Below _____

FORM B: Posttest   Level 6

Sentinels in the Forest

Many wild creatures that travel with their own kind know by instinct how to protect the group. One of them acts as a sentinel.

Hidden by the branches of a low-hanging tree, I once watched two white-tailed deer feeding in a meadow. At first, my interest was held by their beauty. Soon I noticed something quite unusual; they were taking turns feeding. While one was calmly cropping grass, unafraid and at ease, the other—with head high, eyes sweeping the sea marsh and sensitive nostrils "feeling" the air—stood on guard against enemies. Not for a moment, during the half hour I spied upon them, did they stop their teamwork.

Student Responses

Low - High   (Circle number)
1   2   3

PREDICTION:
Picture and Title   1   2   3
What will this story be about?

_____

_____

_____

RETELLING:
Character(s)   1   2   3
This story is not about a person. Can you tell about the animals in the story?

_____

_____

_____

Problem(s)   1   2   3
Tell about what the animals were doing.

_____

_____

_____

Outcome(s)/Solution(s)   1   2   3
Do you think the animals were good at what they were doing? Tell me more about it.

_____

_____

_____

SCORING GUIDE

TOTAL SCORE _____

		Prompting	Comfortable Reading Level
10–12	Comprehension excellent	None _____	
6–9	Comprehension needs assistance	General _____	Above _____
5 or less	Comprehension inadequate	Specific _____	Average _____
		Suggestive _____	Below _____

FORM B: Posttest   Level 7

Danger on the Bike Track

All week, Ed Pike, a young race driver, put his BMX (bicycle moto-cross) racer through a series of test runs. Ed was preparing for the biggest race of the year. He was going to race against another top BMX racer named Jimmy Scott.

The race was to take place on a dangerous track with many bumps and sharp turns. Moto-cross bicycles have small wheels and wide tires to help prevent them from slipping in the turns. Ed knew that he needed something special to beat Jimmy. He decided to use a type of tire never used before.

Jimmy complained that Ed's tires were illegal. The race officials checked the tires and said that Ed was able to use them. Ed Pike felt that he was in real danger because Jimmy was angry about the tires. Soon after the race started, Jimmy tried to cut Ed off but missed. Ed gave his BMX full power and pulled ahead of Jimmy and the others. Jimmy should have paid attention to his own skill and his bike's performance and not worry about Ed's new tires.

Student Responses

Low - High   (Circle number)
1   .2   3

PREDICTION:
Picture and Title   1   2   3
Can you tell what the story will be about?

_____

_____

RETELLING:
Character(s)   1   2   3
Who were the main people in the story? Tell all you can about them.

_____

_____

_____

Problem(s)   1   2   3
What things did Ed worry about? Why do you think he felt he was in danger?

_____

_____

_____

Outcome(s)/Solution(s)   1   2   3
How did the story end? Jimmy worried about the wrong things. Why?

_____

_____

_____

SCORING GUIDE

TOTAL SCORE _____		Prompting		Comfortable Reading Level	
10–12	Comprehension excellent	None	_____		
6 – 9	Comprehension needs assistance	General	_____	Above	_____
5 or less	Comprehension inadequate	Specific	_____	Average	_____
		Suggestive	_____	Below	_____

FORM B: Posttest   Level 8

Courage

Courage is the quality people like most and primitive males gauged their manhood by it as do modern adolescents. Civilized people are dazzled by showy courage. An example are the people at Acapulco who dive off a cliff into the sea. Another is the racing car driver or the trapeze artist, or the bystander who runs through flames to save a stranger.

There is a truer courage that is more gallant though almost invisible. It is found in the steadfastness of ordinary people who very matter-of-factly raise children with disabilities. Courage is found in those people who live in never-ending pain and yet do not hate others. It is found in people who, giving up malice and suspicion, teach themselves to relax and trust. It is also found in the quiet acceptance of monotonous jobs that must be done, yet it's the kind of courage people rarely recognize in themselves.

PREDICTION:
Picture and Title   1   2   3
The picture and title are not much help in predicting what this story is about. The story is really about an idea. Tell me what you know about courage.

_____

_____

_____

RETELLING:
Character(s)   1   2   3
The story tells about two types of courage. Can you describe these types of courage?

_____

_____

_____

Problem(s)/Outcomes   1   2   3
What type of courage does the author believe is the truer type of courage? Tell me more about this type of courage.

_____

_____

_____

_____

SCORING GUIDE

TOTAL SCORE _____

10–12	Comprehension excellent	
6–9	Comprehension needs assistance	
5 or less	Comprehension inadequate	

Prompting		Comfortable Reading Level	
None	_____		
General	_____	Above	_____
Specific	_____	Average	_____
Suggestive	_____	Below	_____

f